Microwave Cooking

Microwave Cooking

Beverley Piper

TREASURE PRESS

First published in Great Britain in 1984 by
Octopus Books Limited

This edition published in 1985 by
Treasure Press
Michelin House
81 Fulham Road
London SW3 6RB

© 1985 Octopus Books Limited

Reprinted 1989

ISBN 1 85051 088 1

Printed by Mandarin Offset in Hong Kong

CONTENTS

Introduction

The microwave oven is a seemingly miracle appliance that cooks food far faster than a conventional stove (range) and thaws frozen food almost instantly. Although microwave cookery does call for a new approach to preparing food this book shows you how a wide variety of family meals, as well as more elaborate dishes for entertaining, can be prepared in an amazingly short time.

Microwave ovens have other advantages over conventional cookers (ranges). They are easier to clean, simply wipe over with a warm, damp cloth. They use far less electricity — there is no need to preheat the oven and cooking time is measured in seconds and minutes rather than in minutes and hours — and they can be plugged into any electrical socket without special installation. They are also light enough for one person to carry. This means that the microwave oven can be used in any room of the house and can even be taken to a holiday home.

Another great advantage is that food is generally cooked on a serving dish which eliminates the need to use all those hard-to-clean pots and pans.

HOW THE MICROWAVE OVEN WORKS

Electrical energy is converted into microwaves by the 'magnetron' and these microwaves are then distributed throughout the oven by a stirrer. They reflect off the sides, top and bottom of the oven and pass through the container on which the food is placed, into the food. The microwaves cause the molecules of moisture in the food to vibrate at 450 million times per second. These vibrations cause friction, friction creates heat, and it is this heat that cooks the food.

SAFETY

Microwave ovens use the same type of energy waves as radio and television, they are not radioactive. All microwave ovens are carefully designed to prevent leakage of the microwaves and at least one safety power cut-out device makes it impossible to operate the oven when the door is open.

All ovens should conform to strict safety regulations laid down by the British Electrotechnical Approvals Board (Food and Drug Administration, Department of Health, Education and Welfare, Performance standards for Microwave Radio Frequency Emitting Products and/or the International Microwave Institute). Choose a microwave oven that is made by a reputable manufacturer and that carries a label confirming that it has passed the statutory safety tests.

SELECTING A MICROWAVE OVEN

Care must be taken when selecting any major item for home use and this is especially true when purchasing a microwave oven since constantly evolving technology is creating more choices than ever before. Consider the type of cooking most frequently done in your home and the size of your family before selecting the microwave oven that has features most suited to your needs.

FEATURES

Microwave ovens may be countertop freestanding models. Alternatively, they can be built into a housing unit which also incorporates a traditional oven and sometimes a traditional grill (broiler).

More advanced (and expensive) microwave models have a grill (broiler) or convection system built into them which provides additional browning. These come into operation either manually or automatically _after_ the microwave cooking time has elapsed. They are an added luxury and are not essential if you have a conventional grill (broiler) in your kitchen (see Browning Aids, opposite).

Computerized microwave ovens are fast becoming the norm. These have MEMORY CONTROLS and can be pre-programmed to defrost, stand and cook food at different power levels, automatically changing from one to another if necessary. With some models an entire cooking programme can be stored in the memory for future re-call.

TEMPERATURE PROBES

A temperature probe (or "food sensor") is a useful built-in feature. The probe is connected to a socket in the oven. The point of the probe is inserted into the thickest part of the food to be cooked and the desired "done" temperature is selected. Once this temperature has been reached, the oven will automatically turn off, or reduce its power to a keep-warm heat level. The probe is particularly useful for cooking large roasts but it should be remembered that the probe only registers the temperature of one area of the roast. The more uniform the size of the piece of meat, the more accurate the temperature probe will be. A MICROWAVE MEAT THERMOMETER is a cheaper alternative to the temperature probe and can be purchased inexpensively from hardware or kitchenware stores. It is inserted into the meat either before or after the meat is put into the roasting bag and it is left in place throughout the cooking time where it registers the internal temperature of the meat. The meat should be removed from the microwave oven when the required temperature is reached.

TURNTABLES

A turntable is simply a revolving platform built into the base of the microwave oven which turns automatically when the oven is on ensuring that all areas of the food receive equal microwave exposure.

Although cooking performance is improved with the use of the turntable, it does restrict the size of the cooking utensils which can be used. Cleaning _under_ the turntable may also prove a problem — always check the turntable is easy to remove before buying a microwave oven. Some models can be used without the turntable in place, allowing you to use larger dishes occasionally, while others incorporate a "hidden turntable" which eliminates cleaning problems.

OVEN POWER OUTPUT

The output of a microwave oven is the amount of energy actually available for the cooking. It will always be _less_ than the in-put power stated by the manufacturer since some of the electricity is used by the magnetron to convert the electricity into microwave energy, and some is consumed by the stirrer. Most domestic microwave ovens have an electrical input of 1,000 to 1,500 watts whereas their output ranges from 500 to 700 watts. The wattages will be displayed either on the back plate of the oven on the control panel, or in the accompanying manual. The power output of the oven controls the time it takes to cook the food. This should be taken into account when following microwave recipes. If following a recipe designed for an oven with a power output either higher or lower than the one being used decrease or increase the cooking time accordingly.

OVEN POWER OUTPUT CHART

> The microwave oven used for testing the recipes in this book had an output of 700W.
>
> If your microwave oven has a different power output adjust the cooking time as follows:
>
> ● If using a 500W oven, increase the time by about 40 seconds for each minute given.
>
> ● If using an oven with a 600W output, increase the time by about 20 seconds for each minute given.
>
> ● If using an oven which has an electrical output higher than 700W, the timing must be decreased accordingly. Always undercook rather than overcook. Food can be put back into the oven for extra cooking if necessary but if it is overcooked it will be spoiled.

DEFROST FEATURE

Most microwave ovens incorporate a defrost cycle which brings about the perfect marriage between microwave oven and freezer. Any type of frozen food may be defrosted quickly and evenly.

The Defrost cycle operates in conjunction with the oven timer and while in operation, microwave energy is pulsated on and off within a pre-set time cycle allowing the food to thaw but not cook. It will continue to operate for the pre-selected time.

Always refer to a defrost chart (see page 91) and bear in mind that the larger or more dense the food, the longer it will take to defrost. The defrost cycle may also be used for selected low power cooking.

The defrosting of larger items of food may be speeded up by starting on a power slightly higher than defrost, finishing on defrost, and then allowing a standing time.

If the food has been frozen in a polythene (plastic) bag, half-turn it into a dish and leave the bag on the food during defrosting until the block is sufficiently thawed for the bag to be removed without tearing.

VARIABLE POWER

As the term suggests, this feature enables the user to select different power levels to cook different foods to the highest possible standard.

Variable power operates in a similar fashion to the defrost feature, the electrical energy being pulsated on and off for varying periods of time according to the power level selected.

As stated above, the microwave oven used to test recipes in this book had a 700 Watt power output. It also had a variable power control, giving a choice of eight different power levels. As different manufacturers use different terminology to describe the variable power feature, it is advisable to refer to the instruction manual accompanying your own oven but the following chart enables you to identify the settings used in this book with your own particular oven.

If the microwave oven being used gives only a choice of defrost and Full Power, use Full Power for recipes calling for any power level from power 6 to full power, altering the cooking time accordingly. Use defrost for power levels less than 6, again altering the cooking time accordingly. With a little practice and care, this variable timing procedure will become both easy and highly desirable for excellent cooked food quality.

BROWNING AIDS

The main criticism of the microwave oven is that most models do not brown the food satisfactorily since unless combined with a browning system the outside surface of the food does not crisp, caramelize or brown. This problem can easily be overcome and appetizingly browned food may be produced by one of the following methods:

The use of a browning agent – this can be a mixture of common ingredients like tomato sauce (catsup), a little brown sugar, soy sauce, bottled brown sauce, and concentrated beef or chicken seasonings diluted with a little water or wine. It can be brushed over the surface of some savoury foods before they are cooked adding browness to the finished dish. The browning mixture can be made up in advance and stored, tightly covered, in the refrigerator.

Cakes and puddings which will be rather pale when cooked in the microwave oven may be coloured by the addition of a little liquid gravy browning or caramel.

A browning dish or skillet – this special utensil is lined on the underside with a material which absorbs the microwave energy and becomes extremely hot. The empty dish is preheated for a few minutes in the microwave oven and then used like a frying pan to sear the food. It will surface-brown chops, sausages, steaks, omelettes, bacon, eggs, pancakes; it will even "sauté" potatoes. The browning dish retains this very high temperature for a short time only so you have to work quickly turning the food to brown it evenly. Unlike most dishes used in the microwave oven it is necessary to use oven gloves (hot pads) when handling a heated browning dish. Browning dishes can be used to sear roasts but the joint should be transferred to a standard microwave oven dish for cooking.

The type of browning dish which comes with its own lid will also double as a casserole dish. The meat may be sealed in the preheated dish, the remaining ingredients added and the cooking completed on a low power in the microwave.

A conventional grill (broiler) – food cooked in the microwave oven can be placed under a preheated conventional grill (broiler) to quickly crisp and brown the surface.

VARIABLE POWER CHART

100%		FULL	. 10
90	FULL	REHEAT	9
80		ROAST	8
70		BAKE	7
60			6
50	MEDIUM	MEDIUM	5
40		SIMMER	4
30		DEFROST	3
20	LOW	WARM	2
10		LOW	1

POSITIONING OF FOOD

If cooking food of uneven shape (chops, for example), place the thickest part of the food towards the outside of the dish where microwaves tend to be more dense. When cooking several potatoes or biscuits, arrange them in a ring pattern (like the numbers on the face of a clock), leaving an empty space in the centre. Each item should be turned during cooking. It is advisable to cook a cake in a ring mould (with a hole in the centre) so there is a greater surface area for microwave penetration.

STIRRING AND TURNING

The amount of stirring or turning necessary during the cooking of the recipes in this book will vary depending on how evenly the microwave energy is distributed in your oven. This is something you will learn by trial and error. Quick cooking dishes usually need to be stirred once or twice, while those that require longer cooking (over 10 minutes) may need to be stirred or turned twice (or more) during cooking. As a general rule, food cooked in a microwave oven with a built-in turntable will only need to be turned or stirred once, if at all. Food cooked in models without a turntable may require frequent turning or stirring.

TIMING

The more food put into the microwave oven, the longer the cooking time will be because the microwave energy has to be shared by all the food being cooked. For example, one baking potato cooked alone requires about 5 minutes; three, cooked together, will take about 13 minutes. This timing principle must be remembered when recipes are halved or doubled, as the timing will need to be altered accordingly. In general, when a recipe is doubled, the cooking time should be increased by between one-third and one-half, testing the food after the shorter time. Similarly, when a recipe is halved, the cooking time is also halved.

STANDING OR EQUALIZING TIME

Food continues to cook by conduction after it has come out of the microwave oven so "standing" time allows the temperature to equalize throughout. The larger the piece or quantity of food, the longer the "standing" time required.

Once the principles of microwave cookery are understood, it is easy to estimate how long it will take to cook a complete meal. The food requiring the longest cooking time (probably the meat, see page 88 for roasting times) is cooked first. Then, during its standing time, vegetables, gravy, quick breads and possibly the dessert are cooked. If any of the cooked dishes need to be re-heated before serving simply return them to the oven for a few seconds.

FOODS THAT CANNOT BE COOKED IN A MICROWAVE OVEN

Eggs in their shell   During cooking, pressure builds up inside the shell and the egg is likely to explode. Eggs can be fried, poached or scrambled in the microwave oven.

Deep fat frying   Since the temperature of the frying oil cannot be controlled in a microwave oven it would be dangerous to deep-fat fry. Shallow frying can be done in a microwave oven using either the browning dish or some other suitable container.

Rich fruit cakes   The high proportion of sugar present makes accurate timing difficult but it is possible to achieve a good result if the cake is cooked in a low power setting and then finished off briefly on high power. Allow the cake to cool completely before turning out.

Popovers or Yorkshire Pudding   These foods will not crisp or brown in the microwave oven so are better baked in a conventional oven.

Pastry and filled pies   Filled pies cooked in a microwave oven from a raw state are pale and often soggy so are best cooked conventionally. Cooked filled pies, however, can be successfully reheated in the microwave oven. Unfilled pie shells (or flan shells) may be cooked in the microwave oven, and puff pastry cooks well although it will not be browned. All pastry products reheat well in the microwave oven (see Reheating, page 91).

Meringues   Because of the high sugar content, conventional meringues will not crisp if cooked in a microwave oven. However a stiff fondant made from egg white and icing sugar produces excellent results, shape the fondant into marble sized balls and microwave 4 at a time on full power for 1½ minutes, allow ½ minute standing time.

COOKING CONTAINERS

Microwaves pass straight through the container in which the food is placed and do not heat it so a great variety of materials can be used for cooking in the microwave oven – good quality (heavy gauge) plastic, paper, glass and china. The food in the container, however, becomes very hot and this heat will be transferred to the container so it would not be advisable to cook a casserole in a plastic container because the length of cooking time could produce enough heat within the food product to melt the plastic.

NEVER USE METAL: Metal reflects microwaves so food placed in metal containers, or within aluminium foil, will not cook and the reflected microwaves could damage the magnetron. China or glassware with a metal trim or ring should not be used either.

Some microwave oven manufacturers advise the use of aluminium foil in small quantities, but follow their instructions carefully.

The shape of the container is also important. Round or oval dishes provide the best results, oblong containers should have rounded corners (square corners attract microwave energy and food in these areas may overcook). Food should be spread evenly within the container. Plastic wrap as a food covering is a boon to the microwave oven user as it prevents the surface of the food from drying and eliminates splashing. Normal gauge plastic wrap, available at all supermarkets, is adequate. Cover the food fairly tightly with the plastic wrap and pierce one hole in the centre to allow steam to escape before cooking.

CLEANING

Because the microwave oven cavity does not become hot, cleaning is both quick and easy. Wiping the interior with a soapy cloth, then a dry cloth, is usually all that is necessary. Abrasives like steel wool pads and scouring powders or conventional oven cleaners should never be used as they could damage the microwave oven lining. Clean the microwave oven interior after each major cooking operation so that spilt food does not have a chance to dry onto the surface. If dried-on spills are a problem boil a cup of water in the oven, this creates steam and condensation which loosens the food particles. They can then easily be wiped away.

MICROWAVE COOKING TIPS

● Microwave citrus fruits to increase the yield of juice. Two fruits need 30 seconds on FULL POWER.

● Heat baby food in the glass jar (covers removed) or a small bowl. Heat for about 30 seconds on FULL POWER; stir and test for temperature required.

● Dry herbs from the garden for winter use. Half a cup of parsley placed between 2 sheets of kitchen paper will take about 2 minutes on FULL POWER. Cool and crush before storing in a tightly covered container.

● Heat brandy to flame puddings. A measure in a glass will take 15 seconds on FULL POWER.

● Soften ice cream straight from the freezer. A few seconds on DEFROST makes it easy to scoop.

● Reconstitute concentrated frozen orange juice quickly. Remove from the container, place in a large jug and microwave on FULL POWER for 30–40 seconds. Add cold water according to package directions. Stir and serve.

● Skin tomatoes, peaches or other fruits quickly. Make a cross in the top of each and microwave on FULL POWER for 30 seconds each.

● Make jellies (flavored gelatins) by placing jelly tablet in a large jug with 150ml/¼ pint (⅔ cup) water. Microwave on FULL POWER for 1½ minutes until jelly melts. Stir and add the remaining water required. Chill to set.

● Prove bread dough rapidly on DEFROST until double in size.

● Sterilize jars for jam making. Half fill the jars with water and bring to the boil in the microwave oven.

● Stew fruit – 500g/1 lb takes roughly 5 minutes on FULL POWER. Stir in sugar to taste.

● For speedy "roast" potatoes – place 500g/1 lb peeled potatoes in a mixing bowl with 3 tablespoons of water. Cover with plastic wrap, pierce the wrap, and cook for 5 minutes on FULL POWER. Drain and dry, then brown in preheated deep fat using a conventional cooker.

● Mature an unripe Brie cheese by microwaving for a few seconds on DEFROST. The time depends on the firmness of the cheese.

● Soften hard butter or margarine by microwaving for about 1½ minutes on DEFROST.

● Make hot milk drinks in double-quick time: heat two mugs of milk on FULL POWER for 3 minutes (the handles will remain cool) then stir in the flavouring.

● Always use a large container when cooking liquids, since these expand quickly in a microwave oven.

● Seasoning and spices become more pronounced in foods cooked in a microwave oven, so use them sparingly.

● Take care when removing plastic wrap because there is often a sudden upsurge of steam.

● Food can be reheated in the browning dish in which it has been prepared as long as the base of the browning dish is completely covered with food.

● To test if a plated meal is hot enough to serve feel the base of the plate near the centre; if this is hot, then the meal will be ready.

● To adapt a favourite conventional recipe, allow one-third to one-quarter of the original suggested cooking time. Remember to undercook, rather than overcook.

● Sprinkle meat tenderizer over small less tender cuts of meat and allow to stand for 20–30 minutes before cooking.

Soups & Starters

The microwave oven speeds up the preparation of
fish and meat pâtés, hot or cold soups, fish and egg starters
and even savoury moulds. Most dishes that are to be
served hot can be made a day in advance and reheated in the
microwave oven a few minutes before serving.

Anchovy Eggs

METRIC/IMPERIAL	AMERICAN
butter (for greasing dishes)	butter (for greasing dishes)
4 eggs	4 eggs
2 tablespoons cream cheese	2 tablespoons cream cheese
250ml/8fl oz whipping cream	1 cup whipping cream
2 teaspoons lemon juice	2 teaspoons lemon juice
½ × 45g/1¾oz can anchovy fillets, drained and chopped	½ × 1¾oz can anchovy fillets, drained and chopped
salt and pepper	salt and pepper
paprika pepper to garnish	paprika pepper to garnish

1 Lightly butter 4 ramekin dishes. Break an egg into each dish. Prick the yolk with a cocktail stick (toothpick).
2 Place the cream cheese in a jug and microwave on POWER 3 for 2 minutes, to soften.
3 Beat the cream and lemon juice into the cream cheese. Fold in the chopped anchovy fillets and season with salt and pepper to taste.
4 Divide the cream cheese mixture between the ramekins and sprinkle a little paprika on top of each.
5 Microwave on POWER 4 for 7–8 minutes, rearranging the dishes twice during cooking, if necessary. Allow to stand for 3 minutes before serving.
Serves 4.
Total Microwave Cooking Time: 9–10 minutes

Warming Winter Soup

METRIC/IMPERIAL	AMERICAN
50g/2oz butter	¼ cup butter
1 large leek, finely sliced	1 large leek, finely sliced
2 large carrots, peeled and thinly sliced	2 large carrots, peeled and thinly sliced
1 × 225g/8oz potato, peeled and cubed	1 cup peeled, cubed potato
1 small cauliflower, divided into florets	1 small cauliflower, divided into florets
2 celery stalks, finely chopped	2 celery sticks, finely chopped
1 onion, finely chopped	1 onion, finely chopped
2 rashers streaky bacon, rind removed and chopped	2 fatty bacon slices, rind removed and chopped
1 teaspoon mixed herbs	1 teaspoon mixed herbs
1 litre/1¾ pints well-flavoured beef or chicken stock (boiling)	4¼ cups well-flavored beef or chicken bouillon (boiling)
freshly ground black pepper	freshly ground black pepper

1 Put the butter into a 2.25–2.75 litre/4–5 pint (10–12 cup) mixing bowl and microwave on FULL POWER for 1½ minutes to melt.
2 Stir in the leek, carrots, potato, cauliflower florets, celery, onion and bacon. Mix well.
3 Cover with plastic wrap and pierce. Microwave on FULL POWER for 4 minutes.
4 Stir in the herbs, stock (bouillon) and pepper to taste.
5 Cover with plastic wrap and pierce. Microwave on FULL POWER for 17 minutes, stirring once, half-way through cooking.
6 Allow to stand, covered, for 6 minutes before serving with grated cheese and French bread.
Serves 6.
Total Microwave Cooking Time: 22½ minutes

Chicken and Corn Soup with Croûtons

METRIC/IMPERIAL	AMERICAN
50g/2oz butter	¼ cup butter
50g/2oz plain flour	½ cup all-purpose flour
300ml/½ pint chicken stock	1¼ cups chicken bouillon
450ml/¾ pint milk	2 cups milk
salt and pepper	salt and pepper
½ × 350g/12oz can sweetcorn kernels, drained	½ × 12oz can sweetcorn kernels, drained
100g/4oz cooked chicken meat, chopped	½ cup cooked, chopped chicken meat
2 tablespoons 'top of the milk'	2 tablespoons half-and-half
croûtons to serve (see page 13)	croûtons to serve (see page 13)

1 Place the butter in a 2.25 litre/4 pint (10 cup) mixing bowl and microwave on FULL POWER for 1½ minutes to melt.
2 Gradually stir in the flour, mixing well with a wooden spoon.
3 Stir in the stock (bouillon) and milk. Season with salt and pepper to taste.
4 Microwave on FULL POWER for 7 minutes, stirring once, half-way through cooking.
5 Beat well with a balloon whisk.
6 Stir in sweetcorn and chicken meat with the cream off the milk (half-and-half). Serve immediately, topped with croûtons.
Serves 4.
Total Microwave Cooking Time: 8½ minutes

Anchovy Eggs (far left); Warming Winter Soup (left); Chicken and Corn Soup with Croûtons (below)

Hot Smoked Mackerel Fillets

METRIC/IMPERIAL	AMERICAN
2 smoked mackerel fillets	2 smoked mackerel fillets
1 tablespoon cottage cheese	1 tablespoon cottage cheese
½ teaspoon dried tarragon	½ teaspoon dried tarragon
6 mushroom stalks, finely chopped	6 mushroom stalks, finely chopped
salt and pepper	salt and pepper
a little garlic seasoning or minced garlic (optional)	a little garlic seasoning or minced garlic (optional)
Garnish:	Garnish:
paprika pepper	paprika pepper
lemon slices	lemon slices

1 Lay mackerel fillets on an oval dish, tails to the centre.
2 Mix together cottage cheese, tarragon, mushroom stalks, salt, pepper and garlic, if liked.
3 Arrange on top of the fish, down the centre of each fillet.
4 Cover loosely with plastic wrap and microwave on POWER 7 for 3 minutes. Drain, if necessary.
5 Garnish with paprika and lemon slices. Serve immediately.
Serves 2.
Total Microwave Cooking Time: 3 minutes.

Hot Smoked Mackerel Fillets; Cheese and Salmon Ring Mould; Pappadom Surprises

Cheese and Salmon Ring Mould

METRIC/IMPERIAL	AMERICAN
25g/1oz butter	2 tablespoons butter
25g/1oz plain flour	¼ cup all-purpose flour
salt and pepper	salt and pepper
1 tablespoon tomato purée	1 tablespoon tomato paste
300ml/½ pint milk	1¼ cups milk
1 × 10g/¼oz sachet gelatine	1 × ¼oz sachet gelatin
75g/3oz Edam cheese, grated	¾ cup grated Edam cheese
1 × 215g/7½oz can salmon	1 × 7½oz can salmon

1 First make the sauce. Place butter in a 1 litre/1¾ pint (4¼ cup) jug and microwave on FULL POWER for 1 minute to melt.
2 Stir in flour and salt and pepper. Blend in tomato purée (paste) and milk.
3 Microwave on FULL POWER for 3 minutes.
4 Beat well until smooth.
5 Cool slightly for 5 minutes, add gelatine then beat until dissolved. Beat in cheese.
6 Drain salmon and discard bones. Flake salmon into sauce and mix well.
7 Pour into a wetted 900ml/1½ pint (3¾ cup) ring mould. Cool, then chill until firm.
8 Turn onto a plate. Serve with brown bread and butter and garnish if liked with sliced cucumber and black olives.
Serves 6.
Total Microwave Cooking Time: 4 minutes

Pappadom Surprises

METRIC/IMPERIAL	AMERICAN
4 pappadoms	4 pappadoms
5 rashers streaky bacon, rind removed	4 fatty bacon slices, rind removed
3 hard-boiled eggs (cooked conventionally), finely chopped	3 hard-boiled eggs (cooked conventionally), finely chopped
50g/2oz red Leicester cheese, grated	½ cup grated Cheddar cheese
chopped parsley to garnish	chopped parsley to garnish
yogurt dressing or mayonnaise to serve	yogurt dressing or mayonnaise to serve

1 Put one pappadom in each of four cereal or soup bowls.
2 Arrange in microwave oven, leaving small space in the centre.
3 Microwave on FULL POWER for 2 minutes, until pappadoms puff up. Set aside.
4 Arrange bacon on a double sheet of kitchen paper on a dinner plate. Leave centre of plate free.
5 Microwave on FULL POWER for 3–4 minutes; then cool and crumble or chop.
6 Mix together the eggs, cheese and bacon, and divide mixture between the cooked pappadoms.
7 Garnish with parsley and offer a bowl of yogurt dressing or mayonnaise separately. Serve at once.
Serves 4.
Total Microwave Cooking Time: 4 minutes

Tomato Soup

METRIC/IMPERIAL	AMERICAN
750g/1½lb firm, ripe tomatoes	1½lb firm, ripe tomatoes
25g/1oz butter	2 tablespoons butter
1 small onion, peeled and finely chopped	1 small onion, peeled and finely chopped
1 carrot, peeled and finely chopped	1 carrot, peeled and finely chopped
1 rasher of streaky bacon, rind removed and chopped	1 fatty bacon slice, rind removed and chopped
2 cloves of garlic, peeled and finely chopped	2 cloves of garlic, peeled and finely chopped
1 litre/1¾ pints chicken stock (warm)	4½ cups chicken bouillon (warm)
25g/1oz flour	¼ cup all-purpose flour
salt and pepper	salt and pepper
Garnish:	Garnish:
Toasted Crumbs (see page 59)	Toasted Crumbs (see page 59)
chopped parsley	chopped parsley

1 Prick each tomato with a fork and arrange on an ovenproof glass dish.
2 Microwave on FULL POWER for 3 minutes or until the skins split. (The timing will vary according to the size and ripeness of the tomatoes.)
3 Skin tomatoes and roughly chop flesh. Set aside.
4 Place the butter in a 1.75 litre/3 pint (7½ cup) ovenproof glass bowl and microwave on FULL POWER for 1 minute to melt.
5 Add the onion, carrot, bacon and garlic, and microwave on FULL POWER for 2½ minutes.
6 Add the flour to the onion and bacon mixture and blend.
7 Stir in the tomatoes and warm stock (bouillon), and season to taste with salt and pepper.
8 Microwave on FULL POWER for 8 minutes, then stir.
9 Allow to stand, covered, for 10 minutes, then pass through a sieve (strainer).
10 Sprinkle with toasted crumbs and parsley and serve.
Serves 4.
Total Microwave Cooking Time: 14½ minutes

Croûtons

METRIC/IMPERIAL	AMERICAN
50g/2oz butter	¼ cup butter
1 tablespoon oil	1 tablespoon oil
4 slices from a sliced loaf, crusts removed	4 slices from a sliced loaf, crusts removed

1 Place the butter and oil in a 1.75 litre/3 pint (7½ cup) oval or round casserole and microwave on FULL POWER for 1½ minutes.
2 Cut bread into small cubes and toss into hot butter and oil. Stir to coat.
3 Microwave on FULL POWER for 2 minutes, then stir.
4 Microwave on FULL POWER for 2 minutes and stir again.
5 Allow to stand for 2 minutes before serving.
Drain on kitchen paper.
Serves 4.
Total Microwave Cooking Time: 5½ minutes

Hot Buttered Grapefruit

METRIC/IMPERIAL	AMERICAN
1 large grapefruit	1 large grapefruit
25g/1oz butter, softened	2 tablespoons butter, softened
25g/1oz soft brown sugar	2 tablespoons light brown sugar
1 glacé cherry, halved	1 candied cherry, halved

1 Cut each grapefruit in half and loosen segments. Put each half into a sundae dish.
2 Mix together butter and sugar, and divide between the grapefruit halves.
3 Microwave on FULL POWER for 2 minutes.
4 Serve immediately, garnished with half a cherry.
Serves 2.
Total Microwave Cooking Time: 2 minutes

Liver and Bacon Pâté

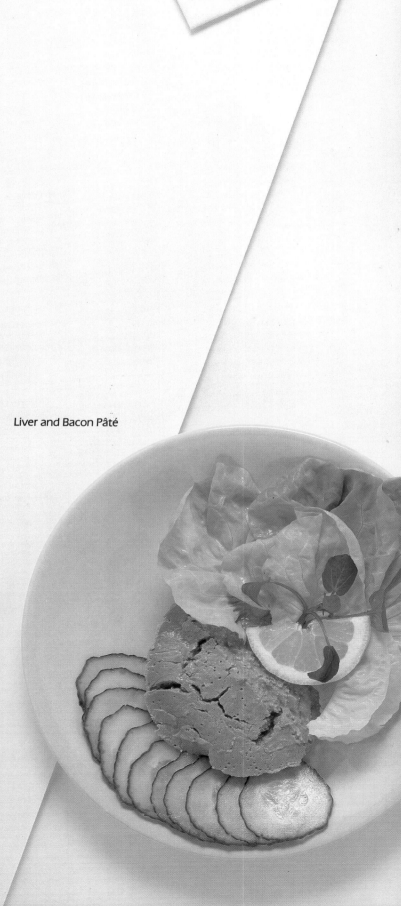

Liver and Bacon Pâté

METRIC/IMPERIAL	AMERICAN
75g/3oz butter	¼ cup plus 2 tablespoons butter
1 onion, finely chopped	1 onion, finely chopped
4 rashers streaky bacon, rind removed and finely chopped	4 fatty bacon slices, rind removed, and finely chopped
500g/1lb chicken livers, washed and roughly chopped	2 cups chicken livers, washed and roughly chopped
1 clove of garlic, chopped (optional)	1 clove of garlic, chopped (optional)
2 bay leaves	2 bay leaves
1 teaspoon lemon juice	1 teaspoon lemon juice
2 tablespoons dry sherry or brandy	2 tablespoons dry sherry or brandy
1 teaspoon dill weed, chopped or dried	1 teaspoon dill weed, chopped or dried
salt and freshly ground black pepper	salt and freshly ground black pepper
150ml/¼ pint whipping cream, whipped until it stands in soft peaks	⅔ cup heavy cream, whipped until it stands in soft peaks
Garnish:	Garnish:
lemon slices	lemon slices
cucumber slices	cucumber slices

1 Put the butter in a 1.75 litre/3 pint (7½ cup) mixing bowl and microwave on FULL POWER for 1½ minutes.
2 Put the onion and bacon into the bowl and stir.
3 Microwave on FULL POWER for 2 minutes.
4 Stir in all remaining ingredients, except the cream. Cover with plastic wrap and pierce.
5 Microwave on POWER 7 for 6 minutes.
6 Remove from microwave oven and rest for 5 minutes. Remove bay leaves and discard.
7 Press through a sieve (strainer) or blend until smooth. Stir well.
8 Stir in cream, and pour into a 900ml/1½ pint (3¾ cup) earthenware dish. Leave to cool.
9 Garnish with slices of lemon and cucumber and serve with crisp lettuce leaves and hot buttered toast.
Serves 6.
Total Microwave Cooking Time: 9½ minutes

Tuna Pâté; Bacon Rolls

Bacon Rolls

METRIC/IMPERIAL
50g/2oz red Leicester cheese, grated
½ × 75g/3oz packet thyme and parsley stuffing, made up according to manufacturer's instructions
12 rashers streaky bacon, rind removed
100g/4oz chicken livers, washed and finely chopped
1 small onion, finely chopped

AMERICAN
½ cup grated Cheddar cheese
½ × 3oz package thyme and parsley stuffing, made up according to manufacturer's instructions
12 fatty bacon slices, rind removed
½ cup chicken livers, washed and finely chopped
1 small onion, finely chopped

1 Mix the cheese into prepared stuffing.
2 Stretch the bacon slices on a chopping board, using the back of a knife, then cut each in half to provide 24 short lengths of bacon.
3 On half of the pieces, spread a little of the stuffing mix.
4 Roll up and secure with a wooden cocktail stick (toothpick).
5 On remaining halves put a piece of chicken liver and a little chopped onion. Roll up as before.
6 Arrange bacon rolls on a double layer of kitchen paper on a dinner plate. Leave a space in the centre.
7 Microwave on FULL POWER for 7–9 minutes.
Serves 6–8 as cocktails.
Total Microwave Cooking Time: 7 minutes

Note: Any remaining filling ingredients can be combined, rolled into balls the size of a walnut, tossed in seasoned flour and cooked.
To Cook: put 1 tablespoon oil in an ovenproof glass pie dish and microwave on FULL POWER for 30 seconds. Add balls of stuffing and microwave FULL POWER for 30 seconds each. Drain and serve.

Tuna Pâté

METRIC/IMPERIAL
100g/4oz butter
2 medium onions, finely chopped
75g/3oz plain flour
300ml/½ pint milk
salt and pepper
2 teaspoons chopped fresh parsley or 1 teaspoon dried
1 × 200g/7oz can tuna fish, drained
3 tablespoons soured cream or natural yogurt
2 teaspoons lemon juice
lemon slices to garnish
To serve:
toast
carrot slices
cucumber slices

AMERICAN
½ cup butter
2 medium onions, finely chopped
¾ cup all-purpose flour
1¼ cups milk
salt and pepper
2 teaspoons chopped fresh parsley or 1 teaspoon dried
1 × 7oz can tuna fish, drained
3 tablespoons sour cream or unflavored yogurt
2 teaspoons lemon juice
lemon slices to garnish
To serve:
toast
carrot slices
cucumber slices

1 Place 50g/2oz butter in a 1 litre/1¾ pint (4¼ cup) jug and microwave on FULL POWER for 1½ minutes to melt.
2 Stir in the onion and microwave on FULL POWER for 2 minutes.
3 Stir in the flour, then gradually stir in milk.
4 Microwave on FULL POWER for 4 minutes.
5 Beat well with a whisk; the sauce will be very thick. Beat in salt and pepper, parsley and remaining butter.
6 Cover with a damp tea (dish) towel and leave to cool for 10 minutes.
7 Flake the fish into a food processor or blender goblet.
8 Add soured cream or yogurt, lemon juice and cooled sauce. Process until smooth.
9 Pour into a serving dish and refrigerate.
10 Garnish with lemon slices and serve with fresh, warm toast and sliced, raw carrots and cucumber.
Serves 6.
Total Microwave Cooking Time: 7½ minutes

Fast Fish

Fish cooks well in the microwave oven but you must
take care not to overcook it. Cook white fish on full power for only 4 to 5 minutes
for each 500 g/1 lb; cook oily fish for 5 to 6 minutes.
Frozen boil-in-the-bag fish dishes can be cooked straight from the freezer
but fish in batter is best cooked conventionally.

Salmon Vol-au-Vent

METRIC/IMPERIAL	AMERICAN
1 × 375g/13oz packet frozen puff pastry, just thawed	1 × 13oz package frozen puff pastry, just thawed
a little milk for brushing	a little milk for brushing
Filling:	Filling:
25g/1oz butter	2 tablespoons butter
25g/1oz plain flour	¼ cup all-purpose flour
salt and pepper	salt and pepper
300ml/½ pint milk	1¼ cups milk
1 × 215g/7½oz can red salmon, drained and flaked	1 × 7½oz can red salmon, drained and flaked
1 tablespoon chopped parsley	1 tablespoon chopped parsley
1 teaspoon fresh lemon juice	1 teaspoon fresh lemon juice

1 Roll the pastry out onto a floured board and into a large circle just over 23cm/9 inches in diameter.
2 Using a 23cm/9 inch plate as a guide, and a sharp knife, cut a circle out of the pastry. Place the circle of pastry upside down on a suitable container.
3 Place an 18cm/7 inch plate gently on top of the pastry and mark round it with a sharp knife, but do not cut right through. On the inner circle, mark an attractive lattice pattern.
4 Brush the pastry with a little milk.
5 Put the vol-au-vent into the refrigerator for 10 minutes.
6 Microwave on FULL POWER for 9-10 minutes, turning the plate once during this time.
7 Allow to stand for 3 minutes, then carefully remove the vol-au-vent 'lid' with a sharp knife.
8 To prepare the filling: place the butter in a 1 litre/1¾ pint (4½ cup) jug and microwave on FULL POWER for 1 minute, to melt.
9 Stir in the flour and salt and pepper. Gradually stir in the milk.
10 Microwave on FULL POWER for 3½ minutes, then beat well.
11 Beat in the salmon, parsley and lemon juice.
12 Put the 'lid' of the vol-au-vent under a preheated very hot grill (broiler). It will brown beautifully in a few seconds.
13 Put the vol-au-vent base on a serving dish. Fill with the sauce, then top with the 'lid'. Serve with a green salad.
Serves 4.
Total Microwave Cooking Time: 14½ minutes

Note: As an alternative, the vol-au-vent can be served cold as a dessert. Fill with whipped cream and strawberries and dredge the top with sifted icing (confectioners') sugar.

Prawns in Cream Sauce

METRIC/IMPERIAL	AMERICAN
225g/8oz sole fillets, skinned	½lb sole fillets, skinned
salt and pepper	salt and pepper
75g/3oz butter	¼ cup plus 2 tablespoons butter
150ml/¼ pint milk plus 1 tablespoon	⅔ cup milk plus 1 tablespoon
1 onion, finely chopped	1 onion, finely chopped
100g/4oz button mushrooms, chopped	1 cup button mushrooms, chopped
25g/1oz plain flour	¼ cup all-purpose flour
150ml/¼ pint dry Vermouth	⅔ cup dry Vermouth
150ml/¼ pint single cream	⅔ cup light cream
225g/8oz peeled prawns	1 cup shelled shrimp
Garnish:	Garnish:
Sprigs of fresh mint	Sprigs of fresh mint
whole prawns	whole shrimp

1 Place the sole in a soup bowl, and season with salt and pepper. Dot with 25g/1oz (2 tablespoons) butter, and pour over 1 tablespoon of milk. Cover with plastic wrap, and pierce.
2 Microwave on FULL POWER for 2 minutes. Set aside.
3 Put 25g/1oz (2 tablespoons) butter and the onion in a 900ml/1½ pint (3¾ cup) bowl. Microwave on FULL POWER for 1 minute. Add the mushrooms, and stir.
4 To make the sauce: place the remaining butter in a 1 litre/1¾ pint (4½ cup) jug and microwave on FULL POWER for 1 minute.
5 Stir in the flour to make a roux. Gradually stir in the dry Vermouth, cream and 150ml/¼ pint/⅔ cup milk. Stir well.
6 Microwave on FULL POWER for 3½ minutes, until the sauce rises nearly to the top of the jug.
7 Beat well with a balloon whisk. Season with salt and pepper.
8 Add the white fish and the prawns (shrimp) to the vegetables, and mix to combine them evenly.
9 Turn into an oval serving dish, and cover with the sauce. Microwave on FULL POWER for 2 minutes.
10 Garnish with mint and prawns (shrimp), and serve with French Potatoes (see page 43) and Cauliflower and Green Bean Salad (see page 52).
Serves 4.
Total Microwave Cooking Time: 9½ minutes

White Fish Crumble

METRIC/IMPERIAL	AMERICAN
½ red pepper, deseeded and finely chopped	½ red pepper, deseeded and finely chopped
25g/1oz butter	2 tablespoons butter
1 tablespoon frozen peas	1 tablespoon frozen peas
500g/1lb sole fillets, skinned and flaked	1lb sole fillets, skinned and flaked
salt and pepper	salt and pepper
2 large, firm tomatoes, peeled and sliced	2 large, firm tomatoes, peeled and sliced
75g/3oz plain crisps, crushed	1½ cups crushed potato chips

1 Place the pepper (reserving a little for garnish) and butter in a 600ml/1 pint (2½ cup) bowl. Microwave on FULL POWER for 1 minute.

2 Add the peas, fish, salt and pepper, and stir.

3 Arrange the tomato slices over the base of an entrée dish. Season with a little salt and pepper.

4 Evenly distribute the fish mixture over the tomatoes, and cover with a lid or plastic wrap. Pierce the plastic wrap, if used.

5 Microwave on FULL POWER for 4 minutes. Remove lid and drain off any surplus liquid.

6 Sprinkle the crisps (potato chips) over the fish, and microwave, uncovered, on FULL POWER for 2 minutes.

7 Serve immediately, garnished with reserved pepper.
Serves 4.
Total Microwave Cooking Time: 7 minutes.

Poached Salmon Steaks

METRIC/IMPERIAL	AMERICAN
150ml/¼ pint chicken stock	⅔ cup chicken bouillon
1 bay leaf	1 bay leaf
salt and pepper	salt and pepper
1 teaspoon lemon juice	1 teaspoon lemon juice
4 salmon steaks (total weight 750g/1½lb), formed into uniform shapes and secured with string	4 salmon steaks (total weight 1½lb), formed into uniform shapes and secured with string
50g/2oz butter	¼ cup butter
Garnish:	Garnish:
lemon quarters	lemon quarters
parsley sprigs or fresh bay leaves	parsley sprigs or fresh bay leaves

1 Place the stock (bouillon), bay leaf, salt and pepper and lemon juice in a 600ml/1 pint (2½ cup) jug. Microwave on FULL POWER for 1½ minutes.

2 Arrange the salmon steaks in a 30 × 20 × 5cm/ 12 × 8 × 2 inch ovenproof glass dish. Pour the stock over, and put 15g/½oz (1 tablespoon) butter onto each salmon steak.

3 Cover with plastic wrap, and pierce. Microwave on FULL POWER for 5–6 minutes, turning steaks over once, half-way through cooking.

4 Stand for 2 minutes before transferring the salmon to a serving dish. Remove string and serve, garnished with lemon, parsley or bay leaves.
Serves 4.
Total Microwave Cooking Time: 6½–7½ minutes

Poached Salmon Steaks (above); Cauliflower and Green Bean Salad (see page 52) (below left); Prawns in Cream Sauce (below right).

Note: The salmon can also be allowed to cool completely in the stock and then lifted out/drained and served cold.
    Use the stock as the base for a sauce to serve with the fish.

18

Seafood Spaghetti

METRIC/IMPERIAL	AMERICAN
1.75 litres/3 pints boiling water	7½ cups boiling water
½ teaspoon salt	½ teaspoon salt
1 tablespoon oil	1 tablespoon oil
225g/8oz spaghetti	½lb spaghetti
1 × 400g/14oz can tomatoes	1 × 14oz can tomatoes
1 tablespoon tomato purée	1 tablespoon tomato paste
100g/4oz peeled prawns	½ cup shelled shrimp
1 × 225g/8oz can crab meat, drained	1 × ½lb can crab meat, drained
12 pimento stuffed olives, drained	12 pimento stuffed olives, drained
salt and pepper	salt and pepper
3 teaspoons cornflour (optional)	3 teaspoons cornstarch (optional)
Garnish:	Garnish:
Parmesan cheese	Parmesan cheese
12 extra pimento olives	12 extra pimento olives

1 Pour 3 pints boiling water into a 2.25 litre/4 pint (10 cup) heatproof mixing bowl. Add salt and oil.
2 Hold the spaghetti in boiling water curling round as the pasta softens, so that all is eventually immersed.
3 Cover with plastic wrap (lift one corner), or a lid, and microwave on FULL POWER for 8 minutes. Set aside, covered.
4 In a large jug put tomatoes, tomato purée (paste), prawns (shrimp), crab meat and olives. Add salt and pepper to taste.
5 Cover with plastic wrap, and pierce. Microwave on FULL POWER for 6 minutes, stirring once, half-way through cooking.
6 Cream the cornflour (cornstarch) to a smooth paste with a little cold water and stir into the hot seafood sauce. Return to the microwave on FULL POWER for 1 minute. Stir.
7 Drain the spaghetti, arrange it on a serving dish and pour over the seafood sauce.
8 Sprinkle liberally with Parmesan cheese, and garnish with olives. Serve with a mixed salad.
Serves 4.
Total Microwave Cooking Time: 15 minutes

Mackerel with Yogurt Sauce

METRIC/IMPERIAL	AMERICAN
4 mackerel (total weight 750g/1½lb), boned and filleted	4 mackerel (total weight 1½lb), boned and filleted
50g/2oz butter	¼ cup butter
salt and pepper	salt and pepper
1 teaspoon dried tarragon	1 teaspoon dried tarragon
1 lemon	1 lemon
Sauce:	Sauce:
1 teaspoon tomato purée	1 teaspoon tomato paste
1 teaspoon lemon juice	1 teaspoon lemon juice
150ml/¼ pint natural yogurt	⅔ cup unflavored yogurt
salt and pepper	salt and pepper
1 teaspoon dried tarragon	1 teaspoon dried tarragon
a few capers	a few capers

1 Arrange the fish, skin side down, in a 30 × 20 × 5cm/12 × 8 × 2 inch ovenproof glass dish.
2 Flake butter evenly over fish. Add salt and pepper to taste and sprinkle over tarragon.
3 Squeeze juice from half the lemon over the fish. Cover with plastic wrap, and pierce.
4 Microwave on FULL POWER for 8 minutes, giving the dish a half-turn, half-way through cooking. Cover and set aside.
5 Meanwhile, prepare the sauce. Blend tomato purée (paste) and lemon juice together, then gradually beat in the yogurt.
6 Add salt and pepper to taste and fold in the tarragon and capers.
7 Serve the fish with a selection of fresh vegetables and hand the cold sauce separately.
Serves 4.
Total Microwave Cooking Time: 8 minutes

Fish in Wine Sauce

METRIC/IMPERIAL	AMERICAN
25g/1oz butter	2 tablespoons butter
25g/1oz plain flour	¼ cup all-purpose flour
salt and pepper	salt and pepper
150ml/¼ pint white wine	⅔ cup white wine
150ml/¼ pint chicken stock	⅔ cup chicken bouillon
50g/2oz mushrooms, thinly sliced	½ cup mushrooms, thinly sliced
350g/12oz white fish, skinned and filleted	¾lb white fish, skinned and filleted
50g/2oz peeled prawns	¼ cup shelled shrimp
1 tomato, sliced	1 tomato, sliced
parsley sprigs to garnish	parsley sprigs to garnish

1 Place the butter in a 1 litre/1¾ pint (4¼ cup) jug, and microwave on FULL POWER for 1 minute.
2 Stir in the flour and salt and pepper to taste. Gradually add the wine and the stock (bouillon), stirring until the ingredients are well mixed. Microwave on FULL POWER for 3½ minutes.
3 Beat with a balloon whisk until sauce is smooth and glossy.
4 Stir in the mushrooms and flaked fish and prawns (shrimp). Stir well.
5 Divide the mixture between individual dishes, or place in a 900ml/1½ pint (3¾ cup) casserole dish. Garnish with tomato slices. Cover with plastic wrap, and pierce.
6 Microwave on POWER 5 for 6 minutes, then garnish with parsley before serving.
Serves 3–4.
Total Microwave Cooking Time: 10½ minutes

Seafood Spaghetti

Trout with Bacon

METRIC/IMPERIAL	AMERICAN
4 trout, cleaned	4 trout, cleaned
8 rashers streaky bacon, rind removed	8 fatty bacon slices, rind removed
1 onion, finely chopped	1 onion, finely chopped
chopped parsley	chopped parsley
salt and pepper	salt and pepper
sprigs of watercress to garnish	sprigs of watercress to garnish

1 Wrap 2 rashers (slices) of bacon neatly round each trout.
2 Arrange fish, compactly, nose to tail in an oblong 900ml/ 1½ pint (3¾ cup) casserole. Make two slight incisions in the side of each fish.
3 Sprinkle the onion and parsley over the fish and season to taste. Cover with plastic wrap, and pierce.
4 Microwave on FULL POWER for 7 minutes, turning trout over once during cooking.
5 Stand for 3 minutes before serving.
6 Garnish with watercress.
Serves 4.
Total Microwave Cooking Time: 7 minutes

Neapolitan Haddock

METRIC/IMPERIAL	AMERICAN
500g/1lb courgettes, washed and sliced	1lb zucchini, washed and sliced
salt	salt
1 × 400g/14oz can chopped tomatoes	1 × 14oz can chopped tomatoes
salt and pepper	salt and pepper
1 teaspoon chopped parsley	1 teaspoon chopped parsley
4 × 85g/3¼oz haddock steaks, defrosted (see page 90)	4 × 3¼oz haddock steaks, defrosted (see page 90)
25g/1oz butter	2 tablespoons butter
25g/1oz Cheddar cheese, grated	¼ cup grated Cheddar cheese
Garnish:	Garnish:
4 black olives	4 ripe olives

1 Arrange the courgettes (zucchini) in a colander, layered with a little salt. Cover with a plate and place a weight on top. Leave for 30 minutes to extract bitter juice.
2 Rinse the courgettes (zucchini) well and place in a 30 × 20 × 5cm/12 × 8 × 2 inch ovenproof glass dish or a shallow 28cm/11 inch round dish. Pour over tomatoes and mix in salt and pepper to taste and chopped parsley.
3 Cover with plastic wrap, and pierce. Microwave on FULL POWER for 9 minutes, stirring once, half-way through cooking. Set aside.
4 Arrange haddock steaks on a dinner plate, towards outer edge.
5 Put a knob of butter on each and sprinkle with salt and pepper.
6 Cover tightly with plastic wrap. Pierce, once, in the centre and microwave on FULL POWER for 3–3½ minutes. Drain.
7 Once the vegetables have completed cooking, and standing, pour off a little of the liquid and reserve to use in a sauce or soup recipe.
8 Arrange haddock on top of vegetables. Sprinkle with cheese and garnish with olives.
9 Microwave on FULL POWER for 1–2 minutes, until the cheese has melted.
Serves 4.
Total Microwave Cooking Time: 14½ minutes

Fish in Soured Cream Sauce

METRIC/IMPERIAL	AMERICAN
4 fillets whiting (total weight about 500g/1lb)	4 fillets whiting (total weight about 1lb)
50g/2oz butter	4 tablespoons butter
2 tablespoons milk	2 tablespoons milk
salt and pepper	salt and pepper
½ red pepper, deseeded and chopped	½ red pepper, deseeded and chopped
150ml/1¼ pint soured cream	⅔ cup sour cream
50g/2oz peeled prawns	¼ cup peeled shrimp
a little dill	a little dill

1 Lay fish fillets in a shallow dish, keeping tails to the centre. Flake half the butter over the fish, add the milk and season with salt and pepper.
2 Cover with plastic wrap and pierce. Microwave on FULL POWER for 4–5 minutes, giving the dish a half turn once during this time.
3 Allow to stand for 5 minutes.
4 Place remaining butter and red pepper into a small jug and microwave on FULL POWER for 30 seconds–1 minute depending on size of the pepper.
5 Stir in soured cream, prawns and dill. Microwave on POWER 4 for 3 minutes. Stir in juices from fish.
6 Arrange fish on a serving dish, pour over the soured cream sauce and garnish with a little extra dill.
Serves 2.
Total Microwave Cooking Time: 9 minutes

Scampi Provençale

METRIC/IMPERIAL	AMERICAN
500g/1lb leeks, well washed and sliced	1lb leeks, well washed and sliced
25g/1oz butter	2 tablespoons butter
1 lemon	1 lemon
2 tablespoons dry cider	2 tablespoons dry cider
50g/2oz mushrooms, washed and sliced	½ cup mushrooms, washed and sliced
1 × 400g/14oz can chopped tomatoes	1 × 14oz can chopped tomatoes
2 teaspoons cornflour	2 teaspoons cornstarch
225g/8oz peeled scampi (defrosted, if necessary)	1 cup peeled jumbo shrimp (defrosted, if necessary)
1 teaspoon chopped parsley	1 teaspoon chopped parsley
salt and pepper	salt and pepper

1 Put the leeks into a 23cm/9 inch pie dish. Do not add any extra water.
2 Cover with plastic wrap, and pierce. Microwave on FULL POWER for 6 minutes. Set to one side.
3 To make the sauce: Place the butter in a 900ml/1½ pint (3¾ cup) mixing bowl and microwave on FULL POWER for 1 minute.
4 Add the juice of half the lemon, the cider, mushrooms and tomatoes, and stir well.
5 Cover with plastic wrap, and pierce. Microwave on FULL POWER for 3 minutes.
6 Mix the cornflour (cornstarch) to a smooth paste with 1 tablespoon cold water. Stir into tomato mixture.
7 Add the scampi (shrimp), parsley and salt and pepper to taste. Microwave on FULL POWER for 1–2 minutes, until the scampi (shrimp) are heated through and the sauce has thickened.
8 Pour over the prepared leeks, and garnish with lemon slices cut from the remaining half lemon.
Serves 2.
Total Microwave Cooking Time: 12 minutes

Scampi Provençale (above);
Neapolitan Haddock (below left);
Fish in Soured Cream Sauce (below)

Hollandaise Sauce

METRIC/IMPERIAL	AMERICAN
50g/2oz butter	¼ cup butter
25g/1oz plain flour	¼ cup all-purpose flour
salt and pepper	salt and pepper
300ml/½ pint milk	1¼ cups milk
1 egg yolk	1 egg yolk
2 tablespoons single cream	2 tablespoons light cream
1 teaspoon lemon juice	1 teaspoon lemon juice

1 Place 25g/1oz (2 tablespoons) butter in a jug and microwave on FULL POWER for about 1 minute, until very hot.
2 Stir in flour and salt and pepper to taste. Stir in milk.
3 Microwave on FULL POWER for 3½ minutes. Beat very well with a balloon whisk, then set aside. (It is important to allow the sauce to stand for a short while before adding the egg yolk and cream as the sauce may curdle if it is too hot.)
4 Beat together the egg yolk and cream, then beat into the slightly cooled sauce. Beat in the remaining butter, a little at a time, and finally stir in the lemon juice.
Serves 3.
Total Microwave Cooking Time: 4½ minutes

Main Meals

Many of the recipes in this section suggest marinading the meat
before cooking and although this will improve the texture and flavour it is not vital.
You can simply paint the meat with a little browning agent
(see Roasting Meat, Page 88) or flash the cooked meat under a preheated grill (broiler).

Sausage Castles

METRIC/IMPERIAL	AMERICAN
500g/1lb pork sausage meat, formed into a roll about 5cm/2 inches in diameter	2 cups pork sausage meat, formed into a roll about 2 inches in diameter
1 egg	1 egg
50g/2oz seasoned plain flour	½ cup seasoned all-purpose flour
1 tablespoon cooking oil	1 tablespoon cooking oil
Sauce:	Sauce:
1 × 400g/14oz can of chopped tomatoes	1 × 14oz can chopped tomatoes
1 small onion, roughly chopped	1 small onion, roughly chopped
1 tablespoon tomato purée	1 tablespoon tomato paste
1 teaspoon soft brown sugar	1 teaspoon brown sugar

1 Cut sausage meat evenly into 6 thick slices. Pat into rounds and coat with egg and seasoned flour.
2 Preheat a browning dish: 4 minutes on FULL POWER for small size; 6 minutes on FULL POWER for a large size.
3 Put oil into the dish and all sausage meat rounds.
4 Microwave on FULL POWER for 2 minutes. Turn rounds over and microwave on POWER 5 for 6 minutes.
5 Remove from microwave oven and transfer to a warmed 30 × 20 × 5cm/12 × 8 × 2 inch ovenproof glass dish. Cover and set aside.
6 To make the sauce: put all sauce ingredients into a blender or food processor. Blend until smooth.
7 Pour into a 1 litre/1¾ pint (4¼ cup) jug and microwave on FULL POWER for 3 minutes.
8 Pass through a sieve onto warm sausage meat rounds.
9 Serve with Jacket Potatoes (see page 52), and peas.
Serves 4.
Total Microwave Cooking Time: 15 or 17 minutes

Pork and Peanut Loaf

METRIC/IMPERIAL	AMERICAN
225g/8oz pork sausage meat	1 cup pork sausage meat
225g/8oz lean minced pork	1 cup lean ground pork
100g/4oz salted peanuts, minced or roughly ground	¾ cup salted peanuts, minced or roughly ground
1 × 50g/2oz packet stuffing mix of choice	1 × 2oz package stuffing mix of choice
1 eating apple, peeled, cored and finely chopped	1 eating apple, peeled, cored and finely chopped
1 medium-sized onion, finely chopped	1 medium-sized onion, finely chopped
freshly ground pepper	freshly ground pepper
1 large egg	1 large egg
redcurrant jelly to glaze	redcurrant jelly to glaze
slices of green and red-skinned apples, dipped in lemon juice, to garnish	slices of green and red-skinned apples, dipped in lemon juice, to garnish

1 Mix together the sausage meat and minced (ground) pork in a 1.75 litre/3 pint (7½ cup) mixing bowl; mix in the nuts.

2 Add all remaining ingredients, except egg, and mix well. Add egg to bind.

3 Press into a non-metallic 1kg/2lb loaf tin.

4 Microwave, uncovered, on POWER 7 for 12 minutes. Allow to rest for 5 minutes before turning out.

5 Glaze with a little redcurrant jelly and garnish with apples. Serve hot or cold with a green salad.

This makes an excellent picnic dish.

Serves 6.

Total Microwave Cooking Time: 12 minutes

Sausage Castles; Meaty Mouthfuls; Pork and Peanut Loaf

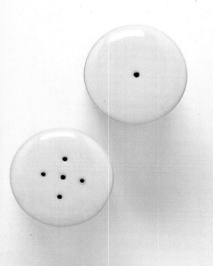

Meaty Mouthfuls

METRIC/IMPERIAL	AMERICAN
350g/12oz minced beef	1½ cups ground beef
225g/8oz pork sausage meat	1 cup pork sausage meat
1 teaspoon mixed herbs	1 teaspoon mixed herbs
50g/2oz fresh white breadcrumbs	1 cup fresh white breadcrumbs
salt and pepper	salt and pepper
1 meat stock cube	2 meat bouillon cubes
1 egg, beaten	1 egg, beaten
1 × 115g/4½oz packet powdered potato (optional garnish)	1 × 4½oz packet powdered potato (optional garnish)
1 × 300g/11oz can tomato soup	1 × 11oz can tomato soup
Parmesan cheese, grated	Parmesan cheese, grated
fresh thyme or rosemary sprigs to garnish	Fresh thyme or rosemary sprigs to garnish

1 First prepare the meat balls. Combine the minced (ground) beef with sausage meat. Mix in the herbs, breadcrumbs, salt and pepper, crumbled stock (bouillon) cube. Bind together with the beaten egg.

2 Roll into 12 meat balls, and arrange on 30 × 20 × 5cm/ 12 × 8 × 2 inch ovenproof glass dish.

3 Cover with plastic wrap, and pierce. Microwave on POWER 7 for 11 minutes.

4 Make up potato as directed on packet.

5 Pipe a border of potato around an entrée dish.

6 Arrange meat balls in centre of dish.

7 Place soup in a 300ml/½ pint (1¼ cup) jug and microwave on FULL POWER for 3 minutes.

8 Pour soup over meat balls, sprinkle with Parmesan.

9 Put the completed dish back in the microwave on FULL POWER for 2 minutes before serving, or brown potato under a preheated hot grill (broiler), if preferred.

10 Garnish with thyme or rosemary.

Serves 4.

Total Microwave Cooking Time: 16 minutes.

Minted Roast Shoulder of Lamb

METRIC/IMPERIAL	AMERICAN
1.5kg/3lb shoulder of lamb (weighed after it has been boned and rolled by the butcher)	3lb shoulder of lamb (weighed after it has been boned and rolled by the butcher)
Garnish:	Garnish:
fresh mint	fresh mint
spring onion curls	scallion curls
Marinade:	Marinade:
150ml/¼ pint dry cider	⅔ cup dry cider
1 teaspoon chopped mint	1 teaspoon chopped mint
1 teaspoon brown sugar	1 teaspoon brown sugar
3 teaspoons soy sauce	3 teaspoons soy sauce
2 tablespoons vinegar	2 tablespoons vinegar
salt and pepper	salt and pepper

1 Place the meat in a large dish. Combine the ingredients for the marinade and pour over the meat. Refrigerate overnight, if possible, basting at least twice.
2 Remove the meat from the marinade and pour off all but about 3 tablespoons of the marinade. Reserve this for the gravy.
3 Sprinkle a little salt over the fat of the meat and put the meat into a roasting bag. Fold the open end under loosely and snip the bag in two or three places to allow the steam to escape.
4 Arrange the meat on an upturned saucer or roasting rack in the base of the roasting dish. Microwave on FULL POWER for 10 minutes.
5 Turn to POWER 8 and microwave for 22 minutes, turning the dish once if necessary.
6 Remove from microwave oven and stand, covered with a 'tent' of foil, for 20 minutes.
7 Uncover meat and place under a preheated grill (broiler) for 10 minutes or until brown and crisp. Garnish with mint and spring onion (scallion) curls and serve.
Serves 6.
Total Microwave Cooking Time: 32 minutes

Note: Lamb should be cooked for 8–9 minutes for each 500g/ 1lb on a high power level.
    It is an excellent idea to make up a basic marinade and keep in a screw-topped jar in the refrigerator.

Crown Roast of Lamb

METRIC/IMPERIAL	AMERICAN
1 × 75g/3oz packet parsley and thyme stuffing	1 × 3oz package parsley and thyme stuffing
1 small egg	1 small egg
50g/2oz mushrooms, sliced	½ cup sliced mushrooms
1 crown roast, about 2kg/ 4½lb when stuffed (this can be ordered and prepared by your butcher)	1 crown roast, about 4½lb when stuffed (this can be ordered and prepared by your butcher)
1 can apricot halves, drained, to garnish	1 can apricot halves, drained, to garnish
Browning agent:	Browning agent:
3 tablespoons tomato sauce	3 tablespoons tomato sauce
1 teaspoon dark brown sugar	1 teaspoon dark brown sugar

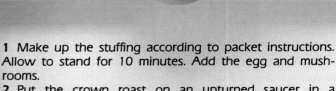

1 Make up the stuffing according to packet instructions. Allow to stand for 10 minutes. Add the egg and mushrooms.
2 Put the crown roast on an upturned saucer in a 30 × 20 × 5cm/12 × 8 × 2 inch ovenproof glass dish. Fill the centre cavity with stuffing.
3 Mix tomato sauce and brown sugar together and brush over the joint and stuffing. Insert microwave meat thermometer between two of the chops.
4 Cover with a split roasting bag and microwave on FULL POWER for 30–40 minutes until the thermometer reads 75°C/170°F.
5 Remove from the oven, cover with a 'tent' of foil and allow to stand until the temperature rises to 82°C/180°F — about 30 minutes.
6 Garnish with apricots and cutlet frills, if liked.
Serves 6.
Total Microwave Cooking Time: 30 minutes.

Roast Loin of Pork

METRIC/IMPERIAL	AMERICAN
1.75g/4lb piece of boned and rolled pork	4lb piece of boned and rolled pork
Marinade:	Marinade:
2 tablespoons wine vinegar	2 tablespoons wine vinegar
2 tablespoons soy sauce	2 tablespoons soya sauce
1 clove of garlic, crushed	1 clove of garlic, crushed
1 teaspoon French mustard	1 teaspoon French mustard
1 teaspoon mixed herbs	1 teaspoon mixed herbs
salt and pepper	salt and pepper
150ml/¼ pint apple juice or pure orange juice	⅔ cup apple juice or pure orange juice
1 sherry glass of dry sherry	1 sherry glass of dry sherry

1 Mix all the ingredients for the marinade together and pour over the meat. Cover the meat and refrigerate for 8 hours, turning the meat three times during this period.

Roast Loin of Pork (left); Minted Roast Shoulder of Lamb (below)

2 Place two upturned saucers, on the base of a 30 × 20 × 5cm/12 × 8 × 2 inch ovenproof glass dish.
3 Drain marinade and retain for gravy.
4 Put the meat into a roasting bag, and fold the open end under. Place in the ovenproof dish and snip the base of the bag in three places.
5 Microwave on FULL POWER for 11 minutes, then give the dish a half-turn.
6 Microwave on POWER 8 for 25 minutes, giving the dish a half-turn, half-way through cooking.
7 Remove from the oven and stand, covered with foil, for 20 minutes.
8 Expose the pork to a preheated hot grill (broiler) for about 12 minutes to 'crisp' the crackling.
9 Serve with baked apples with a mincemeat and nut filling and vegetables of your choice.
Serves 6.
Total Microwave Cooking Time: 36 minutes

Note: A loin of pork should be cooked for 9 minutes for each 500g/1lb.

Gravy

METRIC/IMPERIAL	AMERICAN
40g/1½oz butter	3 tablespoons butter
40g/1½oz plain flour	¼ cup plus 2 tablespoons all-purpose flour
salt and pepper	salt and pepper
1 tablespoon tomato purée (optional)	1 tablespoon tomato paste (optional)
600ml/1 pint well-flavoured stock	2½ cups well-flavored bouillon
Juices from a joint	Juices from a joint

1 Place the butter in a large jug or a 1.75 litre/3 pint (7½ cup) mixing bowl and microwave on FULL POWER for 1 minute.
2 Stir in the flour, salt and pepper, mix well. Microwave on FULL POWER for ½ minute.
3 Gradually mix in tomato purée (paste) and then all the stock (bouillon).
4 Microwave on FULL POWER for 7 minutes, stirring once, half-way through cooking, until boiling.
5 Beat well with a balloon whisk. Beat in the meat juices, and serve.
Serves 4.
Total Microwave Cooking Time: 8½ minutes

Pork Chops with Pineapple

METRIC/IMPERIAL	AMERICAN
1 × 440g/15½oz can pineapple slices in natural juice	1 × 15½oz can pineapple slices in natural juice
6 loin pork chops (total weight 750g/1½lb)	6 loin pork chops (total weight 1½lb)
1 teaspoon made mustard	1 teaspoon made mustard
1 tablespoon soy sauce	1 tablespoon soy sauce
freshly ground black pepper	freshly ground black pepper
1 tablespoon oil	1 tablespoon oil
25g/1oz butter	2 tablespoons butter
2 teaspoons cornflour	2 teaspoons cornstarch

1 Drain pineapple slices and set aside, covered with plastic wrap, in refrigerator.

2 Mix together the mustard, soy sauce and black pepper and gradually stir in the pineapple juice. Pour the mixture over the chops, cover and refrigerate for ½ hour.

3 Preheat a browning dish: 3½ minutes on FULL POWER for small size; 6½ minutes on FULL POWER for the large size. (The chops can be cooked, without soaking, directly onto the preheated skillet, if preferred.)

4 Put the oil, butter and chops into the heated dish.

5 For the large dish: microwave on FULL POWER for 6 minutes; then turn chops over and microwave on FULL POWER for 6 minutes. Arrange chops on a heated serving dish, cover and set aside.

For the small dish: arrange 3 chops on browning dish, and microwave on FULL POWER for 3½ minutes; then turn chops over and microwave on FULL POWER for 3½ minutes. Transfer the chops to a warmed serving dish, cover and set aside. Reheat the browning dish on FULL POWER for 1½ minutes and cook remaining chops in the same way. Set aside.

To complete the dish:

1 Pour the juices in which the chops were soaking into a 600ml/1 pint (2½ cup) jug. Add meat juices.

2 Microwave on FULL POWER for 1½ minutes.

3 Cream the cornflour (cornstarch) with a little water.

4 Pour the heated juices onto the cornflour mix, stirring all the time. Microwave on FULL POWER for 2–3 minutes.

5 Beat the sauce well, pour it over the chops and garnish with pineapple rings.

Serves 6.

Total Microwave Cooking Time: 16½ minutes

Cider Pork Casserole (left); Pork Fillet with Onions (above); Pork Chops with Pineapple (below)

Pork Fillet with Onions

METRIC/IMPERIAL	AMERICAN
2 medium-sized onions, cut into rings	**2 medium-sized onions cut into rings**
1 Bramley cooking apple peeled, cored and sliced	**1 baking apple, peeled, cored and sliced**
25g/1oz butter	**2 tablespoons butter**
750g/1½lb pork fillet, fat removed and cut into 5 × 0.5cm/2 × ¼ inch strips	**1½lb pork tenderloin, fat removed and cut into 2 × ¼ inch strips**
300ml/½ pint boiling chicken stock	**1¼ cups boiling chicken bouillon**
½ teaspoon oregano	**½ teaspoon oregano**
1 tablespoon tomato purée	**1 tablespoon tomato paste**
50g/2oz button mushrooms, wiped and sliced	**½ cup button mushrooms, wiped and sliced**
salt and pepper	**salt and pepper**
3 teaspoons cornflour	**2 teaspoons cornstarch**
Optional Garnish:	Optional Garnish:
thin slices of green pepper julienne (matchstick) strips of raw carrot	**thin slices of green pepper julienne (matchstick) strips of raw carrot**

1 Put the onion and the apple into a 600ml/1 pint (2½ cup) mixing bowl. Cover with plastic wrap, and pierce.
2 Microwave on FULL POWER for 2 minutes.
3 Put the butter in a 30 × 20 × 5cm/12 × 8 × 2 inch oven-proof glass dish. Microwave on FULL POWER for 30 seconds to 1 minute, until the butter has melted and is very hot.
4 Stir in the meat. Microwave on FULL POWER for 2 minutes.
5 Add the apple and onion mixture, stock, oregano, tomato purée (paste), mushrooms and salt and pepper. Stir until all the ingredients are well mixed.
6 Cover with plastic wrap, and pierce. Microwave on FULL POWER for 7 minutes, stirring twice during cooking.
7 Cream the cornflour (cornstarch) with a little water and stir into the pork. Microwave on FULL POWER for 1 minute, and stir.
8 Remove from microwave, cover with a 'tent' of foil, and allow to stand for 12 minutes. Serve with buttered noodles and garnish with green pepper and carrot if liked.
Serves 4.
Total Microwave Cooking Time: 13 minutes

Cider Pork Casserole

METRIC/IMPERIAL	AMERICAN
500g/1¼lb lean pork shoulder, cut into small cubes	**1¼lb lean pork shoulder, cut into small cubes**
300ml/½ pint cider or 300ml/ ½ pint of cider and water mixed	**1¼ cups of cider or 1¼ cups of cider and water mixed**
1½ tablespoons plain flour	**1½ tablespoons all-purpose flour**
salt and pepper	**salt and pepper**
1 medium-sized onion, sliced	**1 medium-sized onion, sliced**
2 carrots, sliced	**2 carrots, sliced**
2 bay leaves	**2 bay leaves**
1 chicken stock cube	**2 chicken bouillon cubes**
squeeze of lemon juice	**squeeze of lemon juice**
50g/2oz mushrooms, sliced	**½ cup sliced mushrooms**
black grapes, halved, to garnish (optional)	**black grapes, halved, to garnish (optional)**

1 Leave meat to soak in the cider or cider and water for ½ hour or overnight.
2 Drain the meat, and reserve the liquid. Toss the meat in the flour seasoned with salt and pepper.
3 Arrange the onion and carrots in a 2 litre/3½ pint (9 cup) casserole.
4 Add the meat, bay leaves, stock (bouillon) cube, lemon juice and reserved liquid.
5 Cover with a lid or plastic wrap. Pierce the plastic wrap, if used, and microwave on FULL POWER for 10 minutes.
6 Stir and microwave on POWER 5 for 30 minutes.
7 Remove bay leaves and stir in the mushrooms. Stand for 10 minutes, covered.
8 Garnish with grapes if liked.
Serves 4.
Total Microwave Cooking Time: 40 minutes

Scalloped Mince Bake

METRIC/IMPERIAL	AMERICAN
500g/1lb minced beef	2 cups ground beef
1 onion, finely chopped	1 onion, finely chopped
1 beef stock cube	2 beef bouillon cubes
1 × 215g/7½oz can baked beans	1 × 7½oz can baked beans
3 tablespoons water or tomato juice	3 tablespoons water or tomato juice
salt and pepper	salt and pepper
500g/1lb potatoes, peeled and thinly sliced	2⅔ cups peeled and thinly sliced potatoes
a little grated cheese	a little grated cheese

1 Place the beef and onion in a 1.75 litre/3 pint (7½ cup) casserole.
2 Stir well and microwave on FULL POWER for 3 minutes.
3 Stir and pour off excess fat. Add the crumbled stock (bouillon) cube, beans and water or tomato juice.
4 Stir and season with salt and pepper. Arrange the potato slices over surface, to cover thinly.
5 Cover with a lid and microwave on POWER 7 for 20 minutes.
6 Sprinkle a little cheese over the potato and return to microwave oven for 2 minutes on FULL POWER to melt, then brown under a preheated grill (broiler).
Serves 4.
Total Microwave Cooking Time: 25 minutes

Scalloped Mince Bake; Fillet Steak Tandoori;
Gammon Steaks with Pineapple

Fillet Steak Tandoori

METRIC/IMPERIAL	AMERICAN
4 fillet steaks	4 fillet steaks
2 tablespoons oil	2 tablespoons oil
Marinade:	Marinade:
275g/10oz natural yogurt	1 cup and 2 tablespoons unflavored yogurt
1 tablespoon paprika pepper	1 tablespoon paprika pepper
1 clove garlic, crushed	1 clove garlic, crushed
3 bay leaves	3 bay leaves
5 peppercorns	5 peppercorns
1 teaspoon salt	1 teaspoon salt
1 tablespoon tomato purée	1 tablespoon tomato paste
1 teaspoon lemon juice	1 teaspoon lemon juice
fresh bay leaves to garnish	fresh bay leaves to garnish

1 Prick the steaks well with a fork and place in a 30 × 20 × 5cm/12 × 8 × 2 inch ovenproof glass dish.
2 Mix all the ingredients for the marinade.
3 Pour the marinade over the steaks, ensuring complete coverage.
4 Cover with plastic wrap and refrigerate overnight.
5 Remove bay leaves and peppercorns and discard.
6 Preheat a browning dish: 4 minutes on FULL POWER for a small size; 7 minutes on FULL POWER for a large size.
7 Put the oil in the dish, then, using a slotted spoon, arrange steaks in dish.
8 Microwave on POWER 8 for 5 minutes, turning the steaks over once, half-way through cooking.
9 Allow to rest for 4 minutes, and garnish with bay leaves. Serve with Fluffy Rice (see page 47) and an orange salad.
Serves 4.
Total Microwave Cooking Time: 5 minutes

Speedy Lemon Liver

METRIC/IMPERIAL	AMERICAN
3 onions, peeled and cut into rings	3 onions, peeled and cut into rings
25g/1oz butter	2 tablespoons butter
350g/12oz lambs' liver, cut into thin strips	¾lb lambs' liver, cut into thin strips
150ml/¼ pint beef stock	⅔ cup beef bouillon
1 teaspoon dried parsley	1 teaspoon dried parsley
1 teaspoon French mustard	1 teaspoon French mustard
2 teaspoons lemon juice	2 teaspoons lemon juice
salt and pepper	salt and pepper
2 teaspoons cornflour	2 teaspoons cornstarch
Garnish:	Garnish:
2 lemon slices	2 lemon slices
chopped parsley	chopped parsley

1 Put the onions in a bowl. Cover with a lid or plastic cling film, pierced.

2 Microwave on FULL POWER for 3 minutes. Set aside.

3 Place the butter in an entrée dish and microwave on FULL POWER for 1 minute.

4 Stir the liver into the hot butter. Cover with plastic wrap and pierce.

5 Microwave on POWER 8 for 3 minutes. Set aside.

6 In a 1 litre/1¾ pint (4¼ cup) jug place the stock (bouillon), parsley, French mustard, lemon juice, and salt and pepper to taste. Microwave on FULL POWER for 2 minutes.

7 Cream cornflour (cornstarch) with a little water to form a smooth paste.

8 Add the juices from the liver to heated stock (bouillon). Beat in the cornflour (cornstarch) and microwave on FULL POWER for 1 minute.

9 To assemble the dish: transfer the liver to a heated plate; rinse the dish and arrange onion rings on base. Top with the cooked liver and pour gravy over.

10 Garnish with lemon slices (cut into a butterfly shape, if wished), and sprinkle with parsley. Serve with Glazed Carrots, (see page 46), sweetcorn, and Jacket Potatoes (see page 52).

Serves 4.

Total Microwave Cooking Time: 10 minutes

Gammon Steaks with Pineapple

METRIC/IMPERIAL	AMERICAN
1 tablespoon cooking oil	1 tablespoon cooking oil
4 gammon steaks (100g/4oz each)	4 ham steaks (¼lb each)
1 × 225g/8oz packet frozen vegetables (sweetcorn and peppers)	1 × 225g/8oz packet frozen vegetables (corn kernels and peppers)
2 processed cheese slices (optional)	2 processed cheese slices (optional)
1 × 225g/8oz can pineapple slices, drained	1 × ½lb can pineapple slices, drained
watercress springs to garnish	watercress sprigs to garnish

1 Preheat a browning dish: 3 minutes on FULL POWER for the small size; 5 minutes on FULL POWER for the large size.

2 Put oil and gammon steaks onto the browning dish and microwave on POWER 7 for 2 minutes.

3 Turn the steaks over and microwave on FULL POWER for 3 minutes.

4 Transfer to a warm serving dish and cover with foil.

5 Pierce the packet of frozen vegetables. Microwave on FULL POWER for 4 minutes and set to one side.

6 If using cheese, cut each slice in half and arrange half a slice on each gammon steak. Top with a pineapple ring and return to the microwave oven on FULL POWER for 2 minutes.

7 Drain the vegetables and arrange on the serving dish with the gammon. Garnish with watercress and serve with creamed potatoes.

Serves 4.

Total Microwave Cooking Time: 12 minutes

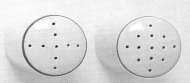

Kidneys in Red Wine

METRIC/IMPERIAL	AMERICAN
50g/2oz butter	¼ cup butter
1 onion, chopped	1 onion, chopped
2 rashers steaky bacon, rinds removed, and chopped	2 fatty bacon slices, rinds removed, and chopped
10 lambs' kidneys, halved and cored	10 lambs' kidneys, halved and cored
1 teaspoon dried tarragon or marjoram	1 teaspoon dried tarragon or marjoram
salt and pepper	salt and pepper
25g/1oz plain flour	¼ cup all-purpose flour
50g/2oz button mushrooms, chopped	½ cup button mushrooms, chopped
150ml/¼ pint red wine	⅔ cup red wine
1 tablespoon soured cream	1 tablespoon sour cream

1 Put the butter into a 1.2 litre/2 pint (5 cup) casserole dish and microwave on FULL POWER for 1½ minutes.
2 Stir in the onion and bacon. Microwave on FULL POWER for 1½ minutes.
3 Stir in the kidneys and tarragon or majoram and season with salt and pepper. Cover with a lid or plastic wrap (pierced) and microwave on FULL POWER for 4 minutes.
4 Stir in the flour, mushrooms and wine. Microwave on FULL POWER for 3 minutes.
5 Stir well, then stand for 5 minutes.
6 Just before serving, swirl a tablespoon of soured cream into the gravy. Serve with Fluffy Rice (page 47).
Serves 4.
Total Microwave Cooking Time: 10 minutes

Buttered Tagliatelle with Parmesan

METRIC/IMPERIAL	AMERICAN
225g/8oz tagliatelle verde	2 cups tagliatelle verde
1 tablespoon oil	1 tablespoon oil
½ teaspoon salt	½ teaspoon salt
2.25 litres/4 pints boiling water	10 cups boiling water
50g/2oz butter	¼ cup butter
1 tablespoon chopped parsley	1 tablespoon chopped parsley
freshly grated Parmesan cheese	freshly grated Parmesan cheese
fresh herbs to garnish	fresh herbs to garnish.

1 Place the tagliatelle, oil and salt in a 2.25 litre/4 pint (10 cup) mixing bowl, and pour over the boiling water.
2 Cover with plastic wrap, and pierce. Microwave on FULL POWER for 6–7 minutes.
3 Allow to stand, covered, for 5 minutes. Then drain the tagliatelle and rinse with boiling water.
4 Pile into a serving dish. Add butter and parsley and toss using a spoon and fork, until tagliatelle is coated.
5 Top with plenty of Parmesan. Garnish with herbs, and serve immediately.
Serves 4.
Total Microwave Cooking Time: 7 minutes

Buttered Tagliatelle with Parmesan (above); Lasagne (below)

Pasta with Bolognese Sauce

METRIC/IMPERIAL
175g/6oz pasta shells
900ml/1½ pints boiling water
1 teaspoon salt
1 tablespoon oil
Bolognese Sauce
1 tablespoon oil
4 rashers streaky bacon, rind removed, and chopped
1 onion, finely chopped
500g/1lb lean minced beef
50g/2oz mushrooms, chopped
1 teaspoon chopped parsley
1 beef stock cube, crumbled
1 teaspoon French mustard
1 teaspoon dried oregano
1 × 225g/8oz can tomatoes, chopped
3 tablespoons tomato purée
1 wine glass red wine
salt and pepper
Garnish:
50g/2oz Parmesan cheese, grated

AMERICAN
1½ cups pasta shells
3¾ cups boiling water
1 teaspoon salt
1 tablespoon oil
Bolognese Sauce
1 tablespoon oil
4 fatty bacon slices, rind removed, and chopped
1 onion, finely chopped
2 cups lean ground beef
½ cup chopped mushrooms
1 teaspoon chopped parsley
2 beef bouillon cubes, crumbled
1 teaspoon French mustard
1 teaspoon dried oregano
1 × 8oz can tomatoes, chopped
3 tablespoons tomato paste
1 wine glass red wine
salt and pepper
Garnish:
½ cup freshly grated Parmesan cheese

1 Place the pasta in a 1.75 litre/3 pint (7½ cup) ovenproof glass mixing bowl. Pour over the boiling water.
2 Add salt and oil, cover with plastic wrap, and pierce. Microwave on FULL POWER for 10 minutes.
3 Remove from microwave oven, stir. Allow to stand, covered with a clean tea (dish) towel, for 5 minutes. Drain.
Bolognese Sauce
1 Preheat a browning dish without its lid: 3 minutes on FULL POWER for the small size: 5 minutes on FULL POWER for the large size.
2 Stir in the oil, bacon and onion. Cover with lid and microwave on FULL POWER for 3 minutes
3 Add the minced beef and stir. Microwave on FULL POWER for 3 minutes.
4 Add all the remaining ingredients and stir well. Microwave on POWER 4 for 20 minutes, covered with the lid.
5 Arrange the drained pasta on a serving dish and pour the sauce over. Sprinkle with grated cheese and serve.
Serves 4.
Total Microwave Cooking Time: 26 minutes.

Lasagne

METRIC/IMPERIAL
2 tablespoons vegetable oil
1 onion, peeled and finely chopped
1 clove of garlic, peeled and crushed
350g/12oz lean minced beef
1 × 225g/8oz can peeled tomatoes
50g/2oz mushrooms, chopped
1 beef stock cube
½ teaspoon dried oregano
2 tablespoons tomato purée
salt and pepper
12 sheets of quick-cooking lasagne
Toasted Crumbs (see page 59)
grated Parmesan cheese
Sauce:
50g/2oz butter
50g/2oz plain flour
600ml/1 pint milk
1 teaspoon made mustard
salt and pepper
75g–100g/3–4oz Mozzarella cheese, grated

AMERICAN
2 tablespoons vegetable oil
1 onion, peeled and finely chopped
1 clove of garlic, peeled and crushed
1½ cups lean ground beef
1 × 8oz can peeled tomatoes
½ cup chopped mushrooms
1 beef bouillon cube
½ teaspoon dried oregano
2 tablespoons tomato paste
salt and pepper
12 sheets quick-cooking lasagne
Toasted Crumbs (see page 59)
grated Parmesan cheese
Sauce:
¼ cup butter
½ cup all-purpose flour
2½ cups milk
1 teaspoon made mustard
salt and pepper
1 cup grated Mozzarella cheese

1 Preheat a browning skillet with its lid on: 3 minutes on FULL POWER for the small size: 5 minutes on FULL POWER for the large size. If a skillet is not available use a large mixing bowl, but do not preheat.
2 Place the oil in the skillet or bowl. Microwave on FULL POWER for 30 seconds.
3 Add the onion, garlic and meat, and stir well. Microwave on FULL POWER for 2 minutes.
4 Stir in the tomatoes, mushrooms, stock (bouillon) cube, oregano and tomato purée (paste). Season well.
5 Put on the lid or cover with plastic wrap, and pierce. Microwave on POWER 7 for 20 minutes. Leave to stand.
To make the sauce:
1 Place the butter in a 2 litre/3½ pint (9 cup) jug or mixing bowl, and microwave on FULL POWER for 1½ minutes.
2 Stir in the flour and half the milk to form a roux. Gradually stir in the remainder of the milk, mustard, and salt and pepper. At this stage the sauce will appear very lumpy.
3 Microwave on FULL POWER for 5 minutes. Beat well. Microwave on FULL POWER for 3 minutes. Beat in the cheese.
To assemble the dish:
1 Grease a 30 × 20 × 5cm/12 × 8 × 2 inch ovenproof glass dish with some melted butter. Cover the base with a little cheese sauce.
2 Arrange three sheets of lasagne over the cheese, cover with a layer of meat and then a layer of cheese sauce.
3 Continue layering in this way until all the ingredients have been used. Finish with a layer of cheese sauce.
4 Sprinkle the top with a few toasted crumbs and a little Parmesan cheese.
5 Cover with plastic wrap, and pierce. Microwave on POWER 8 for 25 minutes. Serve with a green salad.
Serves 4.
Total Microwave Cooking Time: 57 minutes

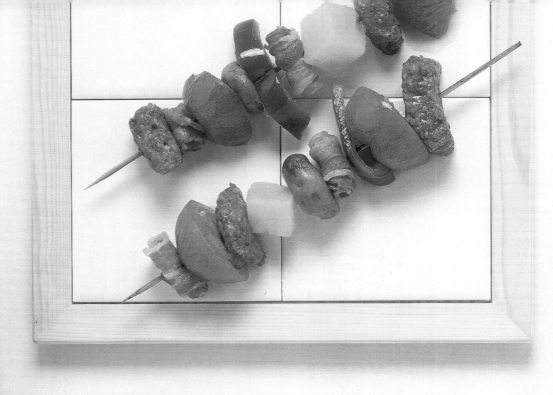

Chilli-Con-Carne

METRIC/IMPERIAL	AMERICAN
1 onion, chopped	1 onion, chopped
2 rashers streaky bacon, rinds removed, and chopped	2 fatty bacon slices, rinds removed, and chopped
500g/1lb lean, raw minced beef	2 cups lean, raw ground beef
1 tablespoon chilli powder	1 tablespoon chilli powder
1 beef stock cube	2 beef bouillon cubes
50g/2oz mushrooms, chopped	½ cup chopped mushrooms
1 teaspoon parsley	1 teaspoon parsley
1 tablespoon chutney	1 tablespoon chutney
1 × 215g/7½oz can kidney beans	1 × 7½oz can kidney beans
2 tablespoons tomato purée	2 tablespoons tomato paste
salt and pepper	salt and pepper
chopped parsley to garnish	chopped parsley to garnish

1 Preheat a browning dish: 3 minutes on FULL POWER for the small size: 5 minutes on FULL POWER for the large size.
2 Put the onion and bacon in the dish, cover with plastic wrap, and pierce. Microwave on FULL POWER for 1 minute.
3 Add beef and stir. Microwave on FULL POWER for 3 minutes.
4 Add all the remaining ingredients and stir well.
5 Cover with lid and microwave on POWER 4 for 30 minutes.
6 Garnish with a little chopped parsley. Serve with a green salad, and French bread, Fluffy Rice, or Jacket Potatoes (see pages 47 and 52).
Serves 3–4.
Total Microwave Cooking Time: 34 minutes

Kebabs

METRIC/IMPERIAL	AMERICAN
9 rashers of streaky bacon, rinds removed	9 fatty bacon slices, rinds removed
4 × 100g/4oz good quality lamb or beef burgers, each cut into 8 pieces.	4 × ¼lb good quality lamb or beef burgers, each cut into 8 pieces
5 firm, medium-sized tomatoes, quartered	5 firm, medium-sized tomatoes, quartered
18 cubes canned pineapple	18 cubes canned pineapple
18 button mushrooms	18 button mushrooms
a few pieces of green pepper	a few pieces of green pepper
rice to serve	rice to serve
6 wooden kebab sticks	6 wooden kebab sticks

1 Stretch out the bacon slices, using the back of a round-bladed knife. Cut each piece in half, and make into 18 rolls.
2 Load each kebab stick with alternating pieces of the prepared food; that is, a bacon roll, a piece of burger, a quarter of a tomato, a piece of pineapple, a mushroom, and the occasional piece of pepper, until all six sticks are full. Leave a small space at each end of each stick.
3 Straddle the loaded kebab sticks widthways across a 30 × 20 × 5cm/12 × 8 × 2 inch ovenproof glass dish. Microwave on FULL POWER for 15 minutes, turning the kebabs and rearranging them twice during cooking.
4 Allow to stand for 4 minutes before serving on a bed of Fluffy Rice (see page 47).
Serves 6.
Total Microwave Cooking Time: 15 minutes
Note: Metal kebab sticks may be used in this recipe *provided* almost all of the metal is masked by the food. The metal must not come into contact with the sides of the oven.

Kebabs; Orange-Stuffed Veal Roll

Orange-Stuffed Veal Roll

METRIC/IMPERIAL	AMERICAN
100g/4oz fresh breadcrumbs	2 cups fresh breadcrumbs
50g/2oz suet, shredded	6 tablespoons shredded suet
25g/1oz raisins	3 tablespoons raisins
salt and pepper	salt and pepper
1 tablespoon pure orange juice	1 tablespoon pure orange juice
2 eggs	2 eggs
1.75kg/4lb breast of veal, boned and rolled	4lb breast of veal, boned and rolled
25g/1oz butter	2 tablespoons butter
2 tablespoons marmalade	2 tablespoons marmalade
Garnish:	Garnish:
slices of orange	slices of orange

1 To make up the stuffing: mix together the breadcrumbs, suet, raisins, salt and pepper, orange juice and the eggs.
2 Lay the veal flat and spread the stuffing over it. Roll up the veal and tie with thin string at 2.5cm/1inch intervals all along the length.
3 Place the butter in a small bowl and microwave on FULL POWER for 30 seconds. Brush the melted butter over the veal, and sprinkle over a little salt.
4 Put the veal into a roasting bag and arrange, on an unturned saucer, in a 30 × 20 × 5cm/12 × 8 × 2 inch oven-proof glass dish.
5 Snip the bag at its base in three places, and microwave on FULL POWER for 10 minutes. Microwave on POWER 8 for 26 minutes, turning the joint over and round half-way through cooking.
6 Allow to stand, covered with a 'tent' of foil for 15–20 minutes.
7 Uncover meat and place under a preheated hot grill (broiler) to brown the top.
8 Place the marmalade in a small jug and microwave on FULL POWER for 1 minute. Sieve and use to glaze meat.
9 Garnish with orange slices.
Serves 6.
Total Microwave Cooking Time: 37½ minutes

Note: Breast of veal is cooked for 8–9 minutes for each 500g/1lb. It is a good idea to use a microwave meat thermometer. Insert the thermometer into the centre of the meat before it goes into the roasting bag. Remove the meat from the microwave oven when the thermometer reads 65°C/149°F.

Crispy Gammon Joint

METRIC/IMPERIAL	AMERICAN
1 piece middle cut or corner of green gammon, about 2kg/4lb, soaked in water overnight	1 smoked ham (rump portion), about 4lb, soaked in water overnight
1 tablespoon honey	1 tablespoon honey
75g/3oz demerara sugar mixed with 1 teaspoon dry mustard	½ cup light brown sugar mixed with 1 teaspoon dry mustard
cloves	cloves
glacé cherries, halved (optional)	candied cherries, halved (optional)

1 Put the drained gammon (ham) into a roasting bag with the honey.
2 Arrange on an upturned saucer in a round casserole dish. Slit the roasting bag at the base, to enable the steam to escape, and microwave on FULL POWER for 10 minutes.
3 Turn the joint over and microwave on POWER 8 for 26 minutes, giving the dish a half-turn, twice, during cooking.
4 Allow to stand, covered with a 'tent' of foil, for 20 minutes.
5 Remove the gammon (ham) and peel away the skin. Score the fat into diamond shapes with a sharp knife and press the sugar and mustard mixture onto the fat. Press a clove into each diamond.
6 Place under a preheated hot grill (broiler) until gammon (ham) is crisp and brown. If liked, decorate the joint with cherries and serve with vegetables of your choice. Delicious hot or cold.
Serves 8–10.
Total Microwave Cooking Time: 36 minutes

Note: If the sugary finish is not liked, the skin can be removed and the fat scored and coated with toasted breadcrumbs. Use the cloves as before.

Rolled Breast of Lamb

METRIC/IMPERIAL	AMERICAN
1.5kg/3lb breast of lamb, boned and rolled	3lb breast of lamb, boned and rolled
Stuffing:	Stuffing:
50g/2oz fresh white breadcrumbs	1 cup fresh white breadcrumbs
2 teaspoons chopped fresh *or* dried mint	2 teaspoons chopped fresh *or* dried mint
1 small onion, finely chopped	1 small onion, finely chopped
25g/1oz shredded suet	3 tablespoons shredded suet
1 egg, beaten	1 egg, beaten
salt and pepper	salt and pepper
Browning agent:	Browning agent:
1 tablespoon tomato sauce mixed with 1 teaspoon dark brown sugar	1 tablespoon tomato sauce mixed with 1 teaspoon dark brown sugar
Garnish:	Garnish:
mint sprigs	mint sprigs
lemon halves	lemon halves

1 To make up the stuffing, mix all ingredients for stuffing together and combine with the egg.
2 Roll out the lamb and spread the stuffing evenly over the entire surface. Re-roll the lamb and tie firmly with string along the length of roll at 2.5cm/1 inch intervals
3 Place two upturned saucers in the base of a 3 × 20 × 5cm/ 12 × 8 × 2 inch ovenproof glass dish.
4 Brush the top of the lamb liberally with the browning agent. Put into a roasting bag, tuck in the end and pierce.
5 Place the joint in the prepared dish and microwave on FULL POWER for 25 minutes. Give the dish a half-turn twice during cooking.
6 Stand, covered in foil, for 20 minutes.
7 Slit the roasting bag to expose the surface of the joint and put under a preheated grill (broiler) for 5 minutes until crisp and brown. Serve immediately with mint and lemon halves.
Serves 4.
Total Microwave Cooking Time: 25 minutes

Note: Cook breast of lamb for 8 minutes per 500g/1lb.

Savoury Sausages

METRIC/IMPERIAL	AMERICAN
1 tablespoon oil	1 tablespoon oil
500g/1lb large pork sausages, pricked	1lb large pork links, pricked

1 Preheat a browning dish: 4 minutes on FULL POWER for the small size; 7 minutes on FULL POWER for the large size.
2 Put the oil and sausages directly into the browning dish, turning and pressing sausages so that all sides have a brief contact with the hot skillet. Do not cover.
3 Microwave on FULL POWER for 1 minute and POWER 5 for 6 minutes. Turn and rearrange sausages once, half-way through cooking.
4 Leave to stand for 2–3 minutes. Serve with Onion Rings (see page 51) and mashed potato.
Serves 4.
Total Microwave Cooking Time: 7 minutes

Veal Speciality

METRIC/IMPERIAL	AMERICAN
8 escalopes of veal (total weight 750g/1½lb)	8 scallops of veal (total weight 1½lb)
25g/1oz fresh breadcrumbs	½ cup of fresh breadcrumbs
1 tablespoon fresh parsley, chopped	1 tablespoon fresh parsley, chopped
50g/2oz button mushrooms, finely chopped	½ cup finely chopped button mushrooms
50g/2oz Edam cheese, finely grated	½ cup finely grated Edam cheese
2 tablespoons mayonnaise	2 tablespoons mayonnaise
salt and pepper	salt and pepper
1 small egg	1 small egg
50g/2oz butter	¼ cup butter
Sauce:	Sauce:
6 tablespoons white wine	6 tablespoons white wine
6 tablespoons well-flavoured veal or chicken stock	6 tablespoons well-flavored veal or chicken bouillon
3 teaspoons cornflour	3 teaspoons cornstarch
salt and pepper	salt and pepper
50g/2oz button mushrooms, sliced	½ cup sliced button mushrooms
1 egg yolk	1 egg yolk
3 tablespoons double cream	3 tablespoons heavy cream
Garnish:	Garnish:
parsley sprigs	parsley sprigs

1 Beat the veal escalopes (scallops) with a meat hammer until each one is very thin.
2 Mix together the parsley, mushrooms, cheese, mayonnaise and salt and pepper. Bind the mixture using the egg.
3 Spread a spoonful of the stuffing on each escalope (scallop). Roll up and secure each one with a cocktail stick (toothpick).
4 Place the butter in a 23cm/9 inch round pie dish and microwave on FULL POWER for 2 minutes until foaming.
5 Put the veal escalopes (scallops) into the dish, turning so that all sides are coated with the hot butter.
6 Cover with plastic wrap, and pierce. Microwave on FULL POWER for 6 minutes, turning escalopes (scallops) over and around, half-way through cooking.
7 Set aside, covered with foil.
8 To make the sauce: put the wine and stock into a small jug in the microwave on FULL POWER for 2 minutes.
9 Cream the cornflour (cornstarch) and salt and pepper with a little water until smooth.
10 Beat the cornflour (cornstarch) into the wine mixture with the juices from the meat. Season with salt and pepper.
11 Microwave on FULL POWER for 1½ minutes, until boiling. Cool slightly and beat in the mushrooms, egg yolk and cream.
12 Arrange the veal in the serving dish. Pour over the sauce and serve garnished with parsley.
Serves 4.
Total Microwave Cooking Time: 11½ minutes

Meat Loaf (above left); Veal Speciality (above right); Rolled Breast of Lamb

Meat Loaf

METRIC/IMPERIAL	AMERICAN
500g/1lb lean minced beef	2 cups lean ground beef
225g/8oz lean bacon, rind removed, and chopped	½lb lean bacon, rind removed, and chopped
50g/2oz fresh breadcrumbs	1 cup fresh breadcrumbs
1 onion, finely chopped	1 onion, finely chopped
1 teaspoon dried parsley	1 teaspoon dried parsley
1 teaspoon dry mustard	1 teaspoon dry mustard
1 tablespoon tomato sauce	1 tablespoon tomato sauce
1 beef stock cube	1 beef bouillon cube
salt and pepper	salt and pepper
2 teaspoons dried peppers	2 teaspoons dried peppers
1 large egg	1 large egg
parsley and red pepper to garnish	parsley and red pepper to garnish
Browning glaze:	Browning glaze:
tomato sauce mixed with 1 teaspoon yeast extract	tomato sauce mixed with 1 teaspoon yeast extract

1 Place beef and bacon in a bowl and work together to combine.

2 Add all remaining ingredients, except the egg, garnish and glaze, and stir well to combine.

3 Add the egg and mix. Press the mixture evenly into a 23 × 13 × 10cm/9 × 5 × 4 inch loaf tin (non metallic).

4 Microwave on POWER 7 for 12 minutes, and turn twice during cooking. Stand, covered loosely with foil, for 5 minutes.

5 Turn out and brush glaze over surface to add colour. Garnish with parsley and red pepper.

Serves 6.

Total Microwave Cooking Time: 12 minutes

**Note: This recipe is delicious hot or cold and can be frozen.
Variation: Slice 50g/2oz cheese thinly and arrange over the surface of the cooked loaf, after the standing time. Return to microwave oven and heat on FULL POWER for 1½ minutes until the cheese has melted. Serve immediately.**

Tempting Turkey

METRIC/IMPERIAL	AMERICAN
3kg/7lb turkey	7lb turkey
25g/1oz butter, melted	2 tablespoons butter, melted
chicken seasoning (used as a browning agent)	chicken seasoning (used as a browning agent)

1 Brush the washed turkey all over with melted butter. Sprinkle with chicken seasoning.
2 Arrange, breast side down, on an up-turned tea plate in a 30 × 20 × 5cm/12 × 8 × 2 inch ovenproof glass dish.
3 Cover with a lid or a split roasting bag. Pierce bag, and microwave on FULL POWER for 12 minutes.
4 Turn turkey the right way up and cook for 1½ hours on POWER 4 or DEFROST . Give the plate a half-turn, three or four times during cooking.
5 Remove from the oven and stand, covered with a 'tent' of foil for 20 minutes before serving.
6 Serve garnished with Bacon Rolls (see page 15), roast potatoes and Brussels sprouts.
Serves 8.
Total Microwave Cooking Time: 1 hour 42 minutes

Note: Turkey is cooked for 14 minutes for each 500g/1lb by this method and is ready when the juices run clear. If preferred, cook on FULL POWER for 7 minutes to the 500g/1lb. Weigh after stuffing.

Your favourite stuffing recipe can be used or try the Chestnut Stuffing below, but add 5 minutes to the cooking time.

Chestnut Stuffing

METRIC/IMPERIAL	AMERICAN
100g/4oz streaky bacon, chopped	¼lb fatty bacon slices, chopped
1 × 500g/1¼lb can whole, peeled chestnuts, drained	1 × 1¼lb can whole, peeled chestnuts, drained
salt and pepper	salt and pepper
100g/4oz fresh brown breadcrumbs	2 cups fresh brown breadcrumbs
25g/1oz butter, melted	2 tablespoons butter, melted
1 teaspoon dried thyme	1 teaspoon dried thyme
1 egg, beaten	1 egg, beaten

1 Put the bacon into a 900ml/1½ pint (3¾ cup) mixing bowl, and microwave on FULL POWER for 2 minutes.
2 Place the chestnuts in a large bowl and mash with a fork.
3 Add the bacon and bacon fat, salt and pepper, bread-crumbs, butter and thyme to the chestnuts. Mix well.
4 Add beaten egg to bind, and use to stuff neck end of bird. Sew up and truss.
5 Proceed to cook turkey as directed above, remembering to allow 5 extra minutes on the cooking time for the bird.
Serves 8.
Total Microwave Cooking Time: 2 minutes

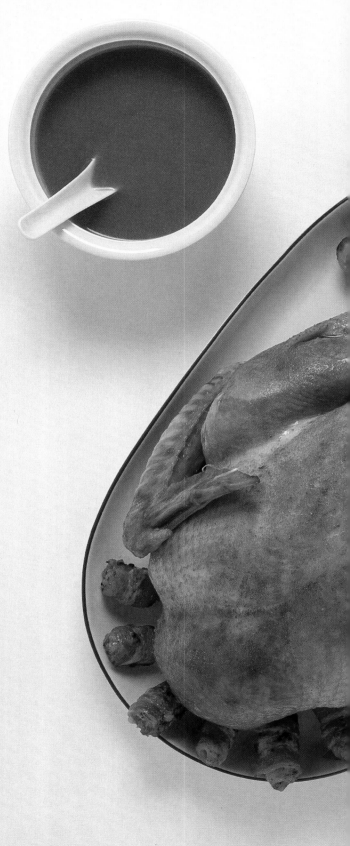

Tempting Turkey with bacon rolls and Brussels sprouts

Roast Chicken

METRIC/IMPERIAL	AMERICAN
25g/1oz butter	2 tablespoons butter
1.5kg/3½lb chicken	3½lb chicken
chicken seasoning	chicken seasoning
(browning agent)	(browning agent)

1 Place the butter in a small container and microwave on FULL POWER for 1 minute.
2 Spread the butter all over the skin of the chicken, then sprinkle liberally with chicken seasoning.
3 Put the chicken into a roasting bag, neck end first. Fold the bag loosely under the bird and pierce the base.
4 Arrange the chicken on an upturned saucer in a 30 × 20 × 5cm/12 × 8 × 2 inch ovenproof glass dish. microwave on FULL POWER for 24 minutes.
5 Remove from microwave oven and cover the bird with a 'tent' of foil, shiny side inwards. Stand for 20 minutes before carving.
Serves 4.
Total Microwave Cooking Time: 25 minutes

Note: Chicken is cooked for 7 minutes for each 500g/1lb. The bird can be stuffed with Mushroom Stuffing (see below), or according to taste but allow an extra 5 minutes cooking time.

Mushroom Stuffing

METRIC/IMPERIAL	AMERICAN
25g/1oz butter	2 tablespoons butter
75g/3oz mushrooms, chopped	1 cup chopped mushrooms
50g/2oz white breadcrumbs	1 cup white breadcrumbs
grated rind of 1 lemon	grated rind of 1 lemon
1 teaspoon dried tarragon	1 teaspoon dried tarragon
salt and pepper	salt and pepper
1 small egg	1 small egg

1 Put the butter into a small bowl and microwave on FULL POWER for 1 minute.
2 Stir in the mushrooms, breadcrumbs, lemon rind and tarragon and salt and pepper to taste.
3 Add the beaten egg, stir to combine and use to stuff the neck end of the bird. Sew up and truss.
4 Proceed to cook chicken as directed above, remembering to allow 5 extra minutes on the cooking time for the bird.
Serves 4.

Total Microwave Cooking Time: 1 minute

Hawaiian Chicken

METRIC/IMPERIAL	AMERICAN
1 onion, peeled and chopped	1 onion, peeled and chopped
2 tablespoons curry powder	2 tablespoons curry powder
1 tablespoon oil	1 tablespoon oil
1 tablespoon plain flour	1 tablespoon all-purpose flour
450ml/¾ pint chicken stock	2 cups chicken bouillon
2 tablespoons apricot jam or chutney	2 tablespoons apricot jelly or chutney
salt and pepper	salt and pepper
1 apple, cored and chopped	1 apple, cored and chopped
1 banana, sliced	1 banana, sliced
25g/1oz sultanas	3 tablespoons golden raisins
100g/4oz frozen mixed vegetables	2 cups frozen mixed vegetables
500g/1lb cooked chicken meat, chopped	2 cups cooked, chopped chicken meat
100g/4oz drained pineapple rings, chopped	2 rings drained pineapple, chopped
To serve:	To serve:
rice	rice
cucumber	cucumber
desiccated coconut	shredded coconut

1 Place the onion, curry powder and oil in a 2.25 litre/4 pint (10 cup) casserole, cover with the lid, and microwave on FULL POWER for 2 minutes.
2 Stir in the flour and gradually stir in the stock (bouillon).
3 Add jam (jelly) or chutney, salt and pepper to taste, apple, banana and sultanas (raisins). Stir, and cover with lid.
4 Microwave on FULL POWER for 10 minutes, stirring once, half-way through cooking.
5 Add the frozen vegetables, chicken meat and pineapple.
6 Microwave, covered, on FULL POWER for 5 minutes. Allow to stand for 5 minutes. Serve with rice, cucumber and coconut.
Serves 4.
Total Microwave Cooking Time: 17 minutes

Chicken Paella

METRIC/IMPERIAL	AMERICAN
1 tablespoon cooking oil	1 tablespoon cooking oil
25g/1oz butter	2 tablespoons butter
1 small onion, chopped	1 small onion, chopped
225g/8oz long-grain rice	1½lb long-grain rice
600ml/1 pint chicken stock	2½ cups chicken bouillon
freshly ground black pepper	freshly ground black pepper
225g/8oz frozen mixed vegetables	1 cup frozen mixed vegetables
225g/8oz boned frozen cod steaks, defrosted	½lb boned frozen cod steaks, defrosted
1 × 99g/3½oz can of tuna fish, drained	1 × 3½oz can of tuna fish, drained
4 tomatoes, skinned and roughly chopped	4 tomatoes, skinned and roughly chopped
225g/8oz cooked chicken meat, chopped	1 cup cooked, chopped chicken meat
pinch of saffron	pinch of saffron
few pimento olives, halved, to garnish	few pimento olives halved, to garnish

Fricassée of Chicken

METRIC/IMPERIAL	AMERICAN
25g/1oz butter	2 tablespoons butter
1 onion, finely chopped	1 onion, finely chopped
1½ tablespoons plain flour	1½ tablespoons all-purpose flour
salt and pepper	salt and pepper
300ml/½ pint milk	1¼ cups milk
1 chicken stock cube	2 chicken bouillon cubes
2 tablespoons frozen minted peas	2 tablespoons frozen minted peas
50g/2oz mushrooms, sliced	½ cup sliced mushrooms
2 tablespoons single cream	2 tablespoons light cream
meat taken from 1 × 1.5kg/ 3½lb cooked chicken, cut into pieces	meat taken from 1 × 3½lb cooked chicken, cut into pieces
2 tablespoons canned sweetcorn	2 tablespoons canned corn kernels
Garnish:	Garnish:
Toasted Crumbs, (see page 59)	Toasted Crumbs, (see page 59)
tomato slices	tomato slices

1 Place the butter in a 1 litre/1¾ pint (4¼ cup) jug, and microwave on FULL POWER for 1 minute.
2 Add the onion and microwave on FULL POWER for 1 minute.
3 Stir in the flour and salt and pepper and gradually stir in the milk. Microwave on FULL POWER for 3 minutes.
4 Beat well with a balloon whisk until a smooth, glossy sauce results. Beat in the crumbled stock (bouillon) cube and peas. Stir in the mushrooms and add the cream.
5 Put the chicken and sweetcorn into a large mixing bowl. Pour over sauce and mix to coat the chicken.
6 Pour into a 30 × 20 × 5cm/12 × 8 × 2 inch ovenproof glass dish and garnish with the Toasted Crumbs and tomato slices.
7 Reheat on POWER 7 for 4 minutes. Serve with Fluffy Rice (see page 47).
Serves 4.
Total Microwave Cooking Time: 9 minutes

1 Put the oil and butter into a 1.75 litre/3 pint (7½ cup) bowl and microwave on FULL POWER for 1 minute.
2 Add the onion and rice and stir well. Microwave on FULL POWER for 2 minutes.
3 Add boiling stock (bouillon), stir well, and season with pepper. Cover with plastic wrap, and pierce.
4 Microwave on FULL POWER for 10–13 minutes. Stir and set aside, covered.
5 To prepare the frozen vegetables: put the packet on a plate, snip a corner of the packet, microwave on FULL POWER for 4 minutes; then drain.
6 To cook the cod steaks: place the packet on a plate, snip the corner and microwave on FULL POWER for 3 minutes. Drain and chop roughly.
7 Put the rice mixture into a serving dish. Add the tuna fish, cod, tomatoes, chicken, saffron and also the mixed vegetables. Toss to mix.
8 Garnish with the pimento olives. Cover with plastic wrap and pierce.
9 Microwave on FULL POWER for 5 minutes to reheat. Serve immediately with green salad and crusty French bread.
Serves 4.
Total Microwave Cooking Time: 25 minutes

Crispy Chicken Drumsticks

METRIC/IMPERIAL	AMERICAN
1 tablespoon cooking oil	1 tablespoon cooking oil
25g/1oz butter	2 tablespoons butter
1 teaspoon chicken seasoning	1 teaspoon chicken seasoning
Toasted Crumbs (see page 59)	Toasted Crumbs (see page 59)
8 chicken drumsticks, skinned	8 chicken drumsticks, skinned
1 egg, beaten	1 egg, beaten.

1 Place the oil and butter in a 30 × 20 × 5cm/12 × 8 × 2 inch ovenproof glass dish and microwave on FULL POWER for 1 minute. (Make sure the base of the dish is covered with fat.)

2 Mix the chicken seasoning into the cold Toasted Crumbs.

3 Dip the chicken legs into the beaten egg and coat with Toasted Crumbs to cover evenly.

4 Arrange the chicken legs in the heated fat, keeping the thick parts to the outside.

5 Microwave, uncovered, on FULL POWER for 10 minutes, turning over once, half-way through cooking.

6 Stand for 2–3 minutes before serving; or serve cold with a watercress and orange salad.

Serves 8.

Total Microwave Cooking Time: 11 minutes

Chicken Paella; Crispy Chicken Drumsticks

Devilled Chicken Pieces

METRIC/IMPERIAL	AMERICAN
4 chicken breasts, skinned and boned (total weight 500g/1lb)	4 chicken breasts, skinned and boned (total weight 1lb)
25g/1oz butter	2 tablespoons butter
1 tablespoon oil	1 tablespoon oil
Marinade:	Marinade:
2 tablespoons soy sauce	2 tablespoons soy sauce
1 tablespoon tomato purée	1 tablespoon tomato paste
3 tablespoons corn oil	3 tablespoons corn oil
1 clove garlic, crushed	1 clove garlic, crushed
1 teaspoon tarragon	1 teaspoon tarragon

1 Place the chicken pieces in a 2.25 litre/½ gallon (5 pint) ice cream container or other suitable dish. Combine the ingredients for the marinade and pour over the chicken.
2 Cover and refrigerate for 2 hours, turning occasionally.
3 Preheat a browning dish: 5 minutes on FULL POWER for the large size; 3½ minutes on FULL POWER for the small size.
4 Place butter and oil in the browning dish. Microwave on FULL POWER for 30 seconds.
5 Drain chicken pieces using a slotted spoon and place in hot fat. Cover and microwave on FULL POWER for 6 minutes, turning over once, half-way through cooking.
6 Remove from microwave oven, cover, and allow to stand for 5 minutes. Garnish as desired and serve with rice or Slimmers' Ratatouille (see page 53).
Serves 4.
Total Microwave Cooking Time: 6½ minutes

Note: If using the small browning dish it may be necessary to cook the chicken in two batches. If so, microwave the first two pieces of chicken for 3 minutes in the preheated dish. Remove these and set aside. Reheat dish for 1 minute on FULL POWER and then proceed as before.

Oriental Chicken

METRIC/IMPERIAL	AMERICAN
1 × 440g/15½oz can pineapple pieces	1 × 15½oz can pineapple pieces
juice of half an orange	juice of half an orange
2 tablespoons clear honey	2 tablespoons clear honey
3 tablespoons dry white wine or 2 tablespoons dry sherry	3 tablespoons dry white wine or 2 tablespoons dry sherry
2 teaspoons soy sauce	2 teaspoons soy sauce
25g/1oz raisins	3 tablespoons raisins
salt and pepper	salt and pepper
4 chicken pieces (about 225g/8oz each), skinned	4 chicken pieces (about ½lb each), skinned
50g/2oz butter	¼ cup butter
3 teaspoons cornflour	3 teaspoons cornstarch
25g/1oz flaked almonds	¼ cup flaked almonds

1 Combine the juice drained from the pineapple, orange juice, honey, wine or sherry, soy sauce, raisins and salt and pepper and stir well
2 Arrange the chicken pieces in a large dish. Pour over the sauce and leave, covered with plastic wrap for at least 30 minutes.
3 Place half the butter in a 30 × 20 × 5cm/12 × 8 × 2 inch ovenproof glass dish and microwave on FULL POWER for 1 minute.
4 Drain the chicken pieces, using a slotted spoon, and reserve the sauce.
5 Put the chicken pieces into hot butter and baste.
6 Cover with plastic wrap, and pierce. Microwave on POWER 8 for 15–17 minutes, turning chicken pieces over once, half-way through cooking.
7 Remove from microwave oven, cover with foil, and leave to stand.
8 To finish the sauce: blend the cornflour (cornstarch) and a little of the sauce to a smooth paste.
9 Put the remaining sauce into a large jug and microwave on FULL POWER for 2 minutes.
10 Mix in the prepared cornflour (cornstarch) and any juice from the chicken. Microwave on FULL POWER for 2 minutes and beat well.
11 Add the drained pineapple pieces and pour the sauce over the chicken.
12 To toast the almonds: arrange the nuts and remaining butter in a small soup bowl, keeping butter in the centre. Microwave on FULL POWER for 1½ minutes and stir. Microwave on FULL POWER for 1 minute and stir. Put the almonds to one side and they will crisp and colour.
13 Drain on kitchen paper and use to garnish the chicken.
Serves 4.
Total Microwave Cooking Time: 17½ minutes

Oriental Chicken (left); Devilled Chicken Pieces (right); Chicken Cordon Bleu (above right)

Chicken Cordon Bleu

METRIC/IMPERIAL	AMERICAN
4 part-boned chicken breasts, skinned (about 225g/8oz each)	4 part-boned chicken breasts, skinned (about ½lb each)
4 rashers streaky bacon, rinds removed, and finely chopped	4 fatty bacon slices, rinds removed, and finely chopped
50g/2oz button mushrooms, finely chopped	½ cup finely chopped button mushrooms
1 teaspoon chopped parsley	1 teaspoon chopped parsley
salt and pepper	salt and pepper
25g/1oz plain flour	¼ cup all-purpose flour
50g/2oz butter	¼ cup butter
4 Gouda cheese slices	4 Gouda cheese slices
fresh parsley to garnish	fresh parsley to garnish

1 Cut a 'pocket' in each piece of chicken.

2 To prepare the filling: put the bacon in an ovenproof glass jug and microwave on FULL POWER for 1½ minutes.

3 Stir in the mushrooms and parsley, and season with salt and pepper.

4 Use the filling to stuff each chicken breast, then coat them with flour seasoned with salt and pepper.

5 Put the butter in a 30 × 20 × 5cm/12 × 8 × 2 inch ovenproof glass dish, and microwave on FULL POWER for 1½ minutes.

6 Stand the chicken pieces in the dish and brush with melted butter. Cover with plastic wrap, and pierce.

7 Microwave on POWER 7 for 7 minutes. Rearrange the chicken pieces.

8 Baste the chicken, cover again with plastic wrap and microwave on POWER 7 for 7 minutes.

9 Remove the plastic wrap and put the chicken on a serving dish.

10 Wrap one cheese slice round each piece of chicken.

11 Microwave on FULL POWER for 2 minutes. Serve garnished with parsley.

Serves 4.

Total Microwave Cooking Time: 19 minutes

Vegetable Cookery

Vegetables cooked in the microwave oven retain their crisp texture,
colour and nutrients. Do not be tempted to add
more water than is suggested in the recipe or you will lengthen the
cooking time and lose valuable minerals and vitamins.

Broad (Fava) Beans with Water Chestnuts

METRIC/IMPERIAL	AMERICAN
1 × 500g/1lb packet frozen broad beans	1lb package frozen fava beans
2 tablespoons cold water	2 tablespoons cold water
50g/2oz butter	¼ cup butter
1 clove garlic, crushed (optional)	1 clove garlic, crushed (optional)
1 × 225g/8oz can water chestnuts, drained and sliced	1 × 8oz can water chestnuts, drained and sliced

1 Place the broad (fava) beans in a 900ml/1½ pint (3¾ cup) casserole dish with the water and cover with the lid.
2 Microwave on FULL POWER for 8 minutes, stirring once, half-way through cooking. Set aside.
3 Put the butter in a jug and microwave on FULL POWER for 1 minute. Add the chopped garlic, if used.
4 Drain the beans, and add the water chestnuts.
5 Pour over the butter and garlic sauce. Toss to coat.
6 Cover with the lid and microwave on FULL POWER for 1 minute.
Serves 4.
Total Microwave Cooking Time: 10 minutes

French Potatoes

METRIC/IMPERIAL

750g/1½lb potatoes, peeled
and very thinly sliced
1 medium-sized onion, sliced
into rings
40g/1½oz butter
salt and pepper
6 tablespoons milk
a little paprika

AMERICAN

1½lb potatoes, peeled and
very thinly sliced
1 medium-sized onion, sliced
into rings
3 tablespoons butter
salt and pepper
6 tablespoons milk
a little paprika

1 Put the potato slices to soak in cold water.
2 Put the onion rings in a bowl. Cover with plastic wrap, and pierce.
3 Microwave on FULL POWER for 1 minute.
4 Grease a 1.2 litre/2 pint (5 cup) entrée dish with a little of the butter. Layer the drained potatoes and onions in the dish, starting and finishing with the potatoes. Season each layer well with salt and pepper.
5 Pour the milk over the potatoes and dot with the rest of the butter. Sprinkle the top with paprika.
6 Cover with plastic wrap, and pierce. Microwave on FULL POWER for 13 minutes, giving the dish a half-turn twice during cooking.
7 Allow to stand, covered, for 5 minutes before serving.
Serves 4.
Total Microwave Cooking Time: 14 minutes

Note: To brown and crisp the top, flash under a preheated grill (boiler).

Broad Beans with Water Chestnuts; French Potatoes;
Celery with Carrots

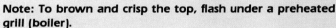

Celery with Carrots

METRIC/IMPERIAL

6 sticks celery, cleaned and
cut into julienne
(matchstick) strips
225g/8oz carrots, scraped
and cut into julienne
(matchstick) strips
25g/1oz butter
1 tablespoon snipped chives
1 teaspoon marjoram
salt and pepper
1 teaspoon chopped parsley

AMERICAN

6 sticks celery, cleaned and
cut into julienne
(matchstick) strips
½lb carrots, scraped and cut
into julienne (matchstick)
strips
2 tablespoons butter
1 tablespoon snipped chives
1 teaspoon marjoram
salt and pepper
1 teaspoon chopped parsley

1 The total weight of the vegetables should be about 350g/12oz. Arrange the celery and carrots in a 900ml/1½ pint (3¾ cup) oval or round casserole dish.
2 Flake the butter over. Sprinkle with chopped chives and marjoram, and season well with salt and pepper.
3 Spoon over 2 tablespoons water. Cover with plastic wrap and pierce.
4 Microwave on FULL POWER for 10 minutes. The vegetables should be stirred half-way through cooking, to make sure that they cook evenly.
5 Allow to stand for 5 minutes, covered. Sprinkle with parsley before serving.
Serves 4.
Total Microwave Cooking Time: 10 minutes

Baked Aubergines

METRIC/IMPERIAL	AMERICAN
2 medium-sized aubergines	2 medium-sized eggplant
salt	salt
225g/8oz cooked, chopped chicken meat	1 cup cooked, chopped chicken meat
1 tablespoon chopped parsley	1 tablespoon chopped parsley
2 tablespoons cooked long-grain rice	2 tablespoons cooked long-grain rice
25g/1oz raisins	3 tablespoons raisins
salt and pepper	salt and pepper
1 tablespoon cream cheese	1 tablespoon cream cheese
2 tablespoons natural yogurt	2 tablespoons unflavored yogurt
50g/2oz Edam cheese, grated	½ cup grated Edam cheese
fresh herbs to garnish	fresh herbs to garnish

1 Halve the aubergines (eggplant) lengthways and scoop out the flesh, leaving a shell 5mm/¼ inch thick. Chop the flesh roughly.
2 Sprinkle the aubergine (eggplant) shells and the pulp with salt and leave to stand for 30 minutes, to extract the excess moisture.
3 Rinse the pulp and shell, drain, and put the pulp into a mixing bowl.
4 Add the chicken, parsley, rice, raisins and salt and pepper.
5 Combine with the cream cheese and yogurt.
6 Pile the mixture back into the aubergine (eggplant) shells. Top with the Edam cheese.
7 Arrange the shells in a 23cm/9 inch round pie dish around outside edge. Cover with plastic wrap, and pierce.
8 Microwave on FULL POWER for 10 minutes. Give the dish a half-turn, twice, during cooking.
9 Allow to stand for 4 minutes and garnish with herbs.
Serves 4.
Total Microwave Cooking Time: 10 minutes

Courgette Boats

METRIC/IMPERIAL	AMERICAN
6 medium-sized courgettes (total weight 850g/1lb 12oz), topped and tailed	6 medium-sized zucchini (total weight 1lb 12oz), topped and tailed
25g/1oz butter	2 tablespoons butter
1 medium-sized onion, finely chopped	1 medium-sized onion, finely chopped
2 large tomatoes, peeled and chopped	2 large tomatoes, peeled and chopped
100g/4oz cooked ham, chopped	½ cup chopped, cooked ham
2 tablespoons fresh white breadcrumbs	2 tablespoons fresh white breadcrumbs
½ teaspoon dried oregano	½ teaspoon dried oregano
salt and pepper	salt and pepper

1 Cut a thin lengthways slice from each courgette (zucchini). Scoop out a channel 1cm/½inch deep. (Keep pulp for a soup recipe.)
2 Place the butter in a jug and microwave on FULL POWER for 1 minute.
3 Stir in the onion. Microwave on FULL POWER for 1 minute.
4 Mix all the remaining ingredients with the cooked onion.
5 Pile evenly into the courgette (zucchini) shells and top with the 'lids'.
6 Arrange the prepared courgette (zucchini) boats in a shallow round container.
7 Pour 2 tablespoons of water into the base, cover tightly with plastic wrap, and pierce once in the centre.
8 Microwave on FULL POWER for 12½ minutes, turning the dish once, half-way through cooking, if necessary.
9 Allow to stand, covered, for 5 minutes. Serve with freshly boiled white or brown rice.
Serves 3.
Total Microwave Cooking Time: 14½ minutes

Broccoli with Piquant Dressing

METRIC/IMPERIAL	AMERICAN
500g/1lb fresh or frozen broccoli spears	1lb fresh or frozen broccoli spears
4 tablespoons water	4 tablespoons water
Dressing:	Dressing:
1 teaspoon tomato purée	1 teaspoon tomato paste
2 teaspoons French mustard	2 teaspoons French mustard
150ml/¼ pint single cream	⅔ cup light cream
1 teaspoon horseradish sauce	1 teaspoon horseradish sauce
1 tablespoon salad cream	1 tablespoon salad cream
salt and pepper	salt and pepper

1 Arrange the broccoli in a shallow oval or round casserole dish, keeping the stalks towards the centre. Using a sharp knife, make two incisions in each stem.
2 Add the water. Cover with plastic wrap, and pierce.
3 Microwave on FULL POWER for 10 minutes, rearranging the broccoli once, half-way through cooking.
4 Allow to stand, covered, while preparing the dressing.
5 To prepare the dressing: mix together the tomato purée (paste) and mustard, and blend in the remaining ingredients.
6 Drain the broccoli, return to the dish. Serve dressing separately.
Serves 4.
Total Microwave Cooking Time: 10 minutes

Courgette Boats; Broccoli with Piquant Dressing; Baked Aubergines

Glazed Carrots

METRIC/IMPERIAL	AMERICAN
500g/1lb carrots, peeled and cut into 5mm/¼ inch slices	1lb carrots, peeled and cut into ¼ inch slices
25g/1oz butter	2 tablespoons butter
2 tablespoons water	2 tablespoons water
1 teaspoon brown sugar	1 teaspoon brown sugar
chopped parsley to garnish	chopped parsley to garnish

1 Pile the carrots into a 900ml/1½ pint (3¾ cup) casserole or vegetable dish.
2 Add the butter and water and sprinkle on the brown sugar.
3 Cover with the casserole lid or plastic wrap. Pierce the wrap, if using, and microwave on FULL POWER for 7 minutes. Baste with the juices.
4 Stand for 3 minutes, covered, and serve sprinkled with chopped parsley.
Serves 4.
Total Microwave Cooking Time: 7 minutes

Mushrooms with Cheese

METRIC/IMPERIAL	AMERICAN
25g/1oz butter	2 tablespoons butter
75g/3oz white breadcrumbs	1½ cups white breadcrumbs
1 clove of garlic, crushed	1 clove of garlic, crushed
225g/8oz mushrooms	2 cups mushrooms
butter for greasing	butter for greasing
pinch of salt	pinch of salt
freshly ground black pepper	freshly ground black pepper
1 small onion, finely chopped	1 small onion, finely chopped
2 tablespoons finely chopped parsley (optional)	2 tablespoons finely chopped parsley (optional)
50g/2oz strong Cheddar cheese, grated	½ cup grated strong Cheddar cheese

1 Put the butter in an ovenproof glass measuring jug and microwave on FULL POWER for 1 minute.
2 Stir in the breadcrumbs and garlic. Microwave on FULL POWER for 3 minutes, stirring once, then set aside.
3 Remove the stalks from the mushrooms (use in a soup or sauce) and place the caps, dark side up, in a lightly greased 23 × 13 × 10 cm/9 × 5 × 4 inch dish.
4 Sprinkle with salt, pepper, onion and parsley, if used.
5 Mix the cheese with the breadcrumbs and sprinkle over the mushrooms.
6 Microwave on FULL POWER for 3–3½ minutes. DO NOT COVER.
Serves 3
Total Microwave Cooking Time: 5 minutes

Note: These mushrooms can be served as a starter or as an accompaniment to a meat dish; they are excellent served with steak.

Rice Salad Ring

METRIC/IMPERIAL
225g/8oz cooked rice (see recipe for Fluffy Rice right)
225g/8oz packet mixed frozen vegetables
salt and pepper

AMERICAN
1½ cups cooked rice (see recipe for Fluffy Rice right)
½lb package mixed frozen vegetables
salt and pepper

1 Prepare the rice according to recipe. Immediately after standing time, place in a sieve and run under cold running water, turning the rice with a fork to separate and cool all the grains.
2 Shake off as much water as possible and place the rice in a large mixing bowl.
3 Place the vegetables, in their packet, on a plate. Pierce the packet, and microwave for 4 minutes on FULL POWER. Drain and rinse under cold running water, until cold.
4 Add the vegetables to the cooked and cooled rice. Toss to mix. Add salt and pepper to taste.
5 Press into a ring mould and refrigerate until required
6 Turn out onto a serving place and fill as required.
Serves 6
Total Microwave Cooking Time: 4 minutes
Variation:
To make Rice Salad: add 25g/1oz (3 tablespoons) raisins, 3 slices of drained, chopped pineapple, and 25g/1oz (¼ cup) roughly chopped walnuts to the cooled rice mixture. Pile onto a bed of lettuce and top with 40g/1½oz peanuts to serve.

Fluffy Rice

METRIC/IMPERIAL
225g/8oz easy cook rice
½ teaspoon salt
15g/½oz butter
650ml/22fl oz boiling water

AMERICAN
1 cup plus 2 tablespoons easy cook rice
½ teaspoon salt
1 tablespoon butter
2¾ cups boiling water

1 Put the rice, salt and butter in a large 1.75 litre/3 pint (7½ cup) mixing bowl. Pour over the boiling water.
2 Cover with plastic wrap, and pierce. Microwave on FULL POWER for 13 minutes. Stir after cooking.
3 Stand, covered, for 10 minutes. Fluff up with a fork and serve.
Serves 4
Total Microwave Cooking Time: 10 minutes

Note: Rice cooks beautifully in the microwave oven. It can be stored in the freezer and reheats well.

Glazed Carrots; Rice Salad Ring; Mushrooms with Cheese

48

Leeks in Wine and Garlic Sauce

1 Place the leeks in a 900ml/1½ pint (3¾ cup) casserole.
2 Cover with the lid or plastic wrap (pierced once) and microwave on FULL POWER for 8 minutes. Stir once during cooking.
3 Set aside and prepare the sauce.
4 Place the butter in a 2 litre/3½ pint (9 cup) jug and microwave on FULL POWER for 1 minute.
5 Stir in the flour, mustard, stock (bouillon) and wine. Add the garlic and salt and pepper.
6 Microwave on FULL POWER for 3½ minutes.
7 Beat well with a balloon whisk. The sauce will thicken while it is being beaten.
8 Pour the sauce over the leeks and sprinkle crumbs liberally over the surface if liked.
9 Reheat on FULL POWER for 2 minutes.
Serves 4.
Total Microwave Cooking Time: 14½ minutes

METRIC/IMPERIAL	AMERICAN
500g/1lb leeks, sliced	1lb leeks, sliced
25g/1oz butter	2 tablespoons butter
25g/1oz plain flour	¼ cup all-purpose flour
1 teaspoon French mustard	1 teaspoon French mustard
150ml/¼ pint chicken stock	⅔ cup chicken bouillon
150ml/¼ pint dry white wine	⅔ cup dry white wine
1 clove garlic, crushed	1 clove garlic, crushed
salt and pepper	salt and pepper
Toasted Crumbs (optional), see page 59	Toasted Crumbs (optional), see page 59

Stuffed Peppers

METRIC/IMPERIAL	AMERICAN
3 large even-sized peppers (about 225g/8oz each)	3 large even-sized peppers (about ½lb each)
2 tablespoons water	2 tablespoons water
1 × 200g/7oz can tuna fish, drained	1 × 7oz can tuna fish, drained
50g/2oz Edam cheese, grated	½ cup Edam grated cheese
1 tablespoon drained canned sweetcorn	1 tablespoon drained canned sweetcorn
2 tablespoons cooked rice	2 tablespoons cooked rice
2 tablespoons mayonnaise	2 tablespoons mayonnaise
salt and pepper	salt and pepper
parsley to garnish (optional)	parsley to garnish (optional)

1 Cut the tops off the peppers and reserve. Scrape out the seeds and discard.
2 Stand the peppers in a 900ml/1½ pint (3¾ cup) oblong casserole and add the water.
3 Cover with plastic wrap or casserole lid. Pierce plastic wrap, if used, and microwave on FULL POWER for 3 minutes.
4 Drain the peppers and set aside.
5 To make the filling: Combine all the remaining ingredients and mix well. Stuff the peppers with the filling.
6 Cover peppers with plastic wrap, pierce and microwave peppers on FULL POWER for 7–8 minutes, then leave to stand for 1 minute. Serve garnished with parsley sprigs if liked.
Serves 3.
Total Microwave Cooking Time: 11 minutes

Note: This recipe is delicious served as an hors d'oeuvres or as an accompaniment to meat.

Leeks in Wine and Garlic Sauce; Stuffed Peppers

Frozen Oven Chips (French Fries)

METRIC/IMPERIAL	AMERICAN
15g/½oz lard or 1 tablespoon oil	1 tablespoon lard or 1 tablespoon oil
175g/6oz frozen oven chips	6oz frozen oven French fries

1 Preheat a deep browning dish: 3 minutes on FULL POWER for the small size; 5 minutes on FULL POWER for the large size.
2 Add the lard or oil and chips (French fries). Stir well.
3 Microwave, uncovered, on FULL POWER for 6 minutes. Stir once after 3 minutes.
4 Stand for 1 minute, then drain on absorbent kitchen paper before serving.
Serves 2
Total Microwave Cooking Time: 6 minutes

Note: To reheat cooked chips (French fries)
Put them into a dish lined with absorbent kitchen paper. Sprinkle with seasoning. Microwave on FULL POWER until very hot, stirring once during cooking. The time taken will depend on the quantity of chips to be reheated.

Corn-on-the-Cob

METRIC/IMPERIAL	AMERICAN
4 frozen corn-on-the-cob	4 frozen corn-on-the-cob
50g/2oz butter	¼ cup butter
4 teaspoons clear honey	4 teaspoons clear honey
salt and pepper	salt and pepper
extra butter to serve	extra butter to serve

1 Arrange the corn in a flan dish.
2 Put 15g/½oz/1 tablespoon of butter and 1 teaspoon of honey on each cob. Season with salt and pepper.
3 Cover with plastic wrap, and pierce. Microwave on FULL POWER for 6 minutes.
4 Rearrange the cobs by turning each one round to face the other way. Baste with juice.
5 Microwave on FULL POWER for 6 minutes.
6 Serve topped with a little extra butter.
Serves 4.
Total Microwave Cooking Time: 12 minutes

Mushrooms in Soured Cream Sauce

METRIC/IMPERIAL	AMERICAN
25g/1oz butter	2 tablespoons butter
1 tablespoon oil	1 tablespoon oil
350g/¾lb button mushrooms, thickly sliced	3 cups thickly sliced button mushrooms
salt and pepper	salt and pepper
150ml/¼ pint soured cream	⅔ cup sour cream
paprika pepper to garnish	paprika pepper to garnish

1 Preheat a browning dish, without a lid: 3 minutes on FULL POWER for the small size; 5 minutes on FULL POWER for the large size.
2 Put the butter and oil into the hot dish, and stir in the mushrooms.
3 Cover with the lid and microwave on FULL POWER for 3 minutes.
4 Strain off the juice and, if wished, reserve for another dish (see Note).
5 Season well with salt and pepper. Stir the soured cream into the mushrooms.
6 Microwave on POWER 4 for 5 minutes.
7 Serve hot or cold sprinkled with paprika.
Serves 4.
Total Microwave Cooking Time: 8 minutes

Note: If Mushrooms in Soured Cream Sauce are to be served with meat or poultry, the juices from the mushrooms can be added to the gravy.

Corn-on-the-Cob; Mushrooms in Soured Cream Sauce;
Cauliflower with Curry Sauce; Onion Rings

Onion Rings

METRIC/IMPERIAL
1 large onion, peeled and
   cut into rings
25g/1oz butter
salt and pepper

AMERICAN
1 large onion, peeled and
   cut into rings
2 tablespoons butter
salt and pepper

1 Put the onion rings into a 900ml/1½ pint (3¾ cup) mixing bowl. Arrange the butter in the centre and season with salt and pepper.
2 Cover with plastic wrap, and pierce. Microwave on FULL POWER for 3 minutes.
3 Stir, then stand 3 minutes before serving.
Serves 4.
Total Microwave Cooking Time: 3 minutes

Cauliflower with Curry Sauce

METRIC/IMPERIAL
1 × 500g/1lb cauliflower
2 tablespoons water
25g/1oz butter
25g/1oz plain flour
1 teaspoon curry powder
1 tablespoon wine vinegar
salt and pepper
300ml/½ pint milk
25g/1oz cheese, grated
   (optional)

AMERICAN
1 × 1lb cauliflower
2 tablespoons water
2 tablespoons butter
¼ cup all-purpose flour
1 teaspoon curry powder
1 tablespoon wine vinegar
salt and pepper
1¼ cups milk
¼ cup grated cheese
   (optional)

1 Remove the outer leaves from the cauliflower and, using an apple corer, remove the centre of the stalk and discard.
2 Wash the cauliflower and place in a large soufflé or pie dish. Add the water.
3 Cover with plastic wrap and release its edge or pierce. Microwave on FULL POWER for 8 minutes, giving the dish a half-turn, half-way through cooking.
4 Remove from microwave and stand, covered, while preparing sauce.
5 To make the sauce: place butter in a 1 litre/1¾ pint (4¼ cup) jug and microwave on FULL POWER for 1 minute.
6 Add the flour, curry powder, wine vinegar and salt and pepper. Gradually stir in the milk.
7 Microwave on FULL POWER for 3 minutes until the sauce rises right to the top of the jug.
8 Remove from the oven then beat well with a balloon whisk.
9 Drain the cauliflower and place in a serving dish. Pour the sauce over cauliflower.
10 Sprinkle with cheese if using and serve immediately.
Serves 3.
Total Microwave Cooking Time: 12 minutes

Cauliflower and Green Bean Salad

METRIC/IMPERIAL	AMERICAN
350g/12oz fresh cauliflower, divided into florets	¾lb fresh cauliflower, divided into florets
5 tablespoons water	⅓ cup water
225g/8oz frozen whole green beans	½lb frozen whole green beans
120ml/4fl oz French dressing	½ cup French dressing
a little fresh, red and green pepper chopped (optional)	a little fresh, red and green pepper, chopped (optional)
finely chopped hard-boiled egg to garnish (optional)	finely chopped hard-cooked egg to garnish (optional)

1 Place the cauliflower florets in a shallow, oval dish, keeping stems to centre.
2 Add 3 tablespoons of the water. Cover tightly with plastic wrap, and pierce.
3 Microwave on FULL POWER for 5–6 minutes. Stir and set aside.
4 Put the beans into a shallow oval dish and add 2 tablespoons of water.
5 Cover tightly with plastic wrap and pierce in centre. Microwave on FULL POWER for 6 minutes, stirring once during cooking. Set aside.
6 Drain the cauliflower and beans. Combine in a bowl and pour over the French dressing.
7 Add the peppers and toss to coat. Cool and then refrigerate.
8 Pile into a serving dish and, if liked, garnish with chopped egg.
Serves 4.
Total Microwave Cooking Time: 12 minutes

Jacket Potatoes

METRIC/IMPERIAL	AMERICAN
4 large potatoes – about 225g/8oz each – scrubbed clean and pricked	4 large potatoes – about ½lb each – scrubbed clean and pricked
2 tablespoons cottage cheese	2 tablespoons cottage cheese
50g/2oz Cheddar cheese, grated	½ cup grated Cheddar cheese
1 canned pineapple ring, chopped	1 canned pineapple ring, chopped
salt and pepper	salt and pepper

1 Arrange the potatoes in a ring on a large dinner plate.
2 Microwave on FULL POWER for 17 minutes, turning the potatoes over once, half-way through cooking.
3 Remove from microwave and stand, covered with a clean tea (dish) towel, for 10 minutes.
4 Mix the cottage cheese, Cheddar cheese, pineapple, salt and pepper.
5 Mark a cross in the top of each potato, and push up from the base to open the potato to form a waterlily shape.
6 Divide the filling between each potato.
Serves 4.
Total Microwave Cooking Time: 17 minutes

New Potatoes with Minted Sauce

METRIC/IMPERIAL	AMERICAN
750g/1½lb new potatoes, cleaned	1½lb new potatoes, cleaned
3 tablespoons water	3 tablespoons water
sprig of fresh mint	sprig of fresh mint
Sauce:	Sauce:
25g/1oz butter	2 tablespoons butter
25g/1oz plain flour	¼ cup all-purpose flour
300ml/½ pint milk	1¼ cups milk
1 teaspoon finely chopped fresh mint	1 teaspoon finely chopped fresh mint
2 tablespoons cream	2 tablespoons cream
salt and pepper	salt and pepper

1 Put the potatoes into a large casserole dish. Add the water and sprig of mint.
2 Cover and microwave on FULL POWER for 10 minutes. Set aside, covered.
3 For the sauce: Put the butter into a 1 litre/1¾ pint (4 cup) jug and microwave on FULL POWER for 1 minute.
4 Stir in the flour and milk then microwave on FULL POWER for 3½ minutes, beating once during this time.
5 Beat in mint, cream and seasoning.
6 Drain potatoes, arrange in a serving dish and pour over the sauce.
Serves 4.
Total Microwave Cooking Time: 14½ minutes

Slimmers' Ratatouille

METRIC/IMPERIAL	AMERICAN
225g/½lb courgettes	½lb zucchini
500g/1lb aubergines	1lb eggplant
salt	salt
1 × 400g/14oz can tomatoes, chopped	1 × 14oz can tomatoes, chopped
½ teaspoon dried basil	½ teaspoon dried basil
salt and pepper	salt and pepper
1 medium-sized onion, finely chopped	1 medium-sized onion, finely chopped
grated Edam cheese to garnish (optional)	grated Edam cheese to garnish (optional)

1 Cut the courgettes (zucchini) and aubergines (eggplant) into 5mm/¼ inch slices and arrange in a colander. Sprinkle with salt. Top with a plate and a weight.
2 Allow to stand for 30 minutes. Rinse well under cold, running water and shake off excess water
3 Layer the courgette (zucchini) and aubergine (eggplant) slices in a 1.75 litre/3 pint (7½ cup) casserole dish, with the tomatoes, basil, salt and pepper and onion. Finish with a layer of tomatoes.
4 Cover with plastic wrap (pierced) or a lid.
5 Microwave on FULL POWER for 20 minutes, turning three times during cooking, if necessary. Remove the lid or plastic wrap for the last 7 minutes to allow some of the liquid to evaporate.
6 Serve hot or cold, sprinkled liberally with grated Edam cheese if liked.
Serves 4.
Total Microwave Cooking Time: 20 minutes

Glazed Sprouts

METRIC/IMPERIAL	AMERICAN
500g/1lb Brussels sprouts	1lb Brussels sprouts
25g/1oz butter	2 tablespoons butter
1 tablespoon lemon juice	1 tablespoon lemon juice
salt and pepper	salt and pepper

1 Peel the sprouts and make a cross in the base of each one.
2 Put into a 900ml/1½ pint (3¾ cup) casserole dish, add the remaining ingredients and stir.
3 Cover with the casserole lid or plastic wrap (pierced). Microwave on FULL POWER for 4 minutes.
4 Stand for 5 minutes before serving.
Serves 3.
Total Microwave Cooking Time: 4 minutes

Note: It is advisable to stir Brussels sprouts once during cooking to help them cook more evenly.

Glazed Sprouts; Slimmers' Ratatouille; New Potatoes with Minted Sauce; Jacket Potatoes

Supper Dishes

The microwave oven enables you to produce instant suppers
for anyone in the family who works late or
arrives home hungry. This is particularly true when the microwave
oven is used in conjunction with a freezer, a prepared
meal can be defrosted and cooked to piping hot perfection in minutes.

Leek and Ham Roll-Ups

METRIC/IMPERIAL	AMERICAN
500g/1lb leeks (two thick leeks), each cut into two widthways	1lb leeks (two thick leeks), each cut into two widthways
2 tablespoons water	2 tablespoons water
25g/1oz butter	2 tablespoons butter
25g/1oz plain flour	¼ cup all-purpose flour
salt and pepper	salt and pepper
1 teaspoon made mustard	1 teaspoon made mustard
300ml/½ pint milk	1¼ cups milk
50g/2oz red Leicester cheese, finely grated	½ cup finely grated double Gloucester cheese
4 slices cooked ham	4 slices cooked ham
Garnish:	Garnish:
Toasted Crumbs (see page 59)	Toasted Crumbs (see page 59)
tomato slices (optional)	tomato slices (optional)

1 Arrange the leeks in a 23cm/9 inch ovenproof glass pie dish.

2 Add the water, cover with plastic wrap, and pierce. Microwave on FULL POWER for 7 minutes.

3 Remove from microwave oven and set aside.

4 To make the sauce: place the butter in a 1 litre/1¾ pint (4¼ cup) jug and microwave on FULL POWER for 1 minute.

5 Stir in the flour to make a roux. Add the salt and pepper and mustard, then gradually add the milk, stirring well.

6 Microwave on FULL POWER for 3 minutes. Remove from oven and beat well. Beat in the grated cheese.

7 Drain the leeks, and roll one slice of ham around each leek.

8 Pour sauce over leeks and ham, sprinkle with Toasted Crumbs and arrange a few tomato slices on top if liked.

9 Reheat on POWER 7 for 5 minutes and serve immediately. Serves 4.

Total Microwave Cooking Time: 16 minutes

Note: This dish freezes well.

Poached Eggs with Peas and Potatoes

METRIC/IMPERIAL	AMERICAN
500g/1lb old potatoes, peeled and diced	1lb old potatoes, peeled and diced
3 tablespoons milk	3 tablespoons milk
salt	salt
4 eggs	4 eggs
1 × 225g/8oz packet frozen peas	1 × ½lb package frozen peas
extra milk for mashing	extra milk for mashing
25g/1oz butter	2 tablespoons butter

1 Put the potatoes into a 1.75 litre/3 pint (7½ cup) mixing bowl. Add the milk and salt.
2 Cover with plastic wrap and pierce. Microwave on FULL POWER for 7—9 minutes, stirring once, if necessary.
3 Stir the potatoes and leave to stand, covered.
4 Put 1 tablespoon water into each of 4 indents in an egg poacher (available for microwave ovens) or into each of 4 cocotte dishes. Microwave on FULL POWER for 1½ minutes, until the water is boiling.
5 Crack an egg into each dish or indent. Prick each yolk with a cocktail stick (toothpick) and microwave for 2—2½ minutes. Set aside.
6 Place peas in their packet in a small casserole dish and pierce the packet.
7 Microwave on FULL POWER for 3 minutes.
8 Meanwhile, mash the potatoes, adding the extra milk as necessary, and the butter.
9 Serve the potato and eggs with the peas.
Serves 4.
Total Microwave Cooking Time: 16 minutes

Variation
To prepare duchesse potatoes: use a forcing bag fitted with a star tube and pipe small pyramids of potato onto a greased tray. Place under a preheated grill (broiler) until 'set', then brush with a little beaten egg and return to grill (broiler) to crisp and brown.

Leek and Ham Roll-Ups; Poached Eggs with Peas and Potatoes

Sausage and Kidney Supper Dish

METRIC/IMPERIAL	AMERICAN
25g/1oz butter	2 tablespoons butter
1 onion, peeled and chopped	1 onion, peeled and chopped
6 lambs' kidneys, skinned, halved and cored	6 lambs' kidneys, skinned, halved and cored
225g/8oz skinless pork sausages, cut into 5cm/2 inch pieces	½lb pork links, cut into 2 inch pieces
25g/1oz plain flour	¼ cup all-purpose flour
1 tablespoon tomato purée	1 tablespoon tomato paste
1 beef stock cube dissolved in 300ml/½ pint water	2 beef bouillon cubes dissolved in 1¼ cups water
1 teaspoon French mustard	1 teaspoon French mustard
salt and pepper	salt and pepper
chopped parsley to garnish	chopped parsley to garnish

1 Place the butter in a 1.75 litre/3 pint (7½ cup) mixing bowl and microwave on FULL POWER for 1 minute.
2 Stir in the onion and kidneys, and microwave on FULL POWER for 2 minutes.
3 Stir in the sausages; cover with plastic wrap and pierce. Microwave on POWER 5 for 7 minutes, then stand for 3 minutes.
4 Using a slotted spoon, transfer the sausages and kidneys to a warm 30 × 20 × 5cm/12 × 8 × 2 inch ovenproof glass dish, and cover with foil.
5 Add the flour and tomato purée (paste) to the onion and fat, and stir.
6 Gradually stir in stock (bouillon) and season with mustard, salt and pepper.
7 Microwave on FULL POWER for 4 minutes.
8 Beat well with a balloon whisk and pour over the sausages and kidneys. Serve garnished with chopped parsley.
Serves 3—4.
Total Microwave Cooking Time: 14 minutes

Cheese and Onion Bake

METRIC/IMPERIAL	AMERICAN
25g/1oz butter	2 tablespoons butter
2 medium-sized onions, cut into rings	2 medium-sized onions, cut into rings
50g/2oz mushrooms, finely chopped	½ cup finely chopped mushrooms
600ml/1 pint milk	2½ cups milk
100g/4oz fresh brown breadcrumbs	2 cups fresh brown breadcrumbs
100g/4oz Cheddar cheese, finely grated	1 cup finely grated Cheddar cheese
salt and pepper	salt and pepper
3 large eggs, beaten	3 large eggs, beaten
1 teaspoon dried dill	1 teaspoon dried dill
paprika pepper	paprika pepper
Optional Garnish:	Optional Garnish:
tomato slices	tomato slices
parsley sprigs	parsley sprigs

1 Put the butter in the base of a 30 × 20 × 5cm/12 × 8 × 2 inch ovenproof glass dish and microwave on FULL POWER for 1 minute.
2 Stir in the onions. Microwave on FULL POWER for 2 minutes. Stir in the mushrooms and set aside.
3 Place the milk in a 1 litre/1¾ pint (4¼ cup) jug and microwave on FULL POWER for 6 minutes.
4 Place the breadcrumbs, cheese and salt and pepper in a 1.75 litre/3 pint (7½ cup) mixing bowl. Pour over hot milk and stir well. Stir in the eggs and dill.
5 Pour onto the onions and mushrooms, and microwave, uncovered, on POWER 7 for 13 minutes. Give the dish a half-turn, twice, during cooking.
6 Sprinkle with paprika and garnish with tomato slices and parsley if using. Allow to stand for 5 minutes before serving.
Serves 4.
Total Microwave Cooking Time: 22 minutes

Beef Burgers

METRIC/IMPERIAL	AMERICAN
1 tablespoon oil	1 tablespoon oil
4 × 100g/4oz beef burgers	4 × ¼lb beef burgers
4 baps or other soft rolls	4 baps or other soft rolls
relish of choice	relish of choice
Onion Rings (see page 51)	Onion Rings (see page 51)

1 Preheat a browning dish: 4 minutes on FULL POWER for the small size; 6 minutes on FULL POWER for the large size.
2 Put the oil onto the heated dish and add beef burgers. Microwave uncovered on FULL POWER for 3 minutes.
3 Turn beef burgers over and microwave on FULL POWER for 3 minutes. Drain on kitchen paper. Split rolls and fill each one with a beef burger.
4 Place filled rolls on a sheet of kitchen paper on a dinner plate and microwave on POWER 5 for 2 minutes.
5 Serve with a relish and onion rings, if liked.
Serves 4.
Total Microwave Cooking Time: 8 minutes

Note: Two 225g/½lb beef burgers, chicken, lamb or pork burgers, can be cooked for the same length of time.

Cheese and Onion Bake;
Wholemeal Pizza served with a mixed salad

Cheese Dreams

METRIC/IMPERIAL	AMERICAN
2 slices of bread, crusts removed	2 slices of bread, crusts removed
1 slice ham	1 slice ham
25g/1oz cheese, grated	¼ cup grated cheese
butter for spreading	butter for spreading
1 tablespoon cooking oil	1 tablespoon cooking oil
25g/1oz margarine	2 tablespoons margarine

1 Make a sandwich with bread, ham, cheese and butter.
2 Preheat a browning dish: 3 minutes on FULL POWER for the small size; 5 minutes on FULL POWER for the large size.
3 Place the oil and margarine in the browning dish. Cover with the lid and microwave on FULL POWER for 1 minute.
4 Remove the lid and put the sandwich in the hot fat. Microwave on FULL POWER for 1 minute.
5 Turn the sandwich over and microwave on FULL POWER for 1 minute.
6 Drain on kitchen paper and serve cut into triangles.
Serves 1.
Total Microwave Cooking Time: 3 minutes

Wholemeal Pizza

METRIC/IMPERIAL	AMERICAN
225g/8oz wholemeal bread dough, (see Wholemeal Plait, page 82)	½lb wholemeal bread dough, (see Wholemeal Plait, page 82)
3 rashers streaky bacon, rind removed and chopped	3 fatty bacon slices, rind removed and chopped
½ × 400g/14oz can tomatoes, chopped	½ × 14oz can tomatoes, chopped
1 tablespoon dried onion	1 tablespoon dried onion
1 teaspoon dried oregano	1 teaspoon dried oregano
1 teaspoon mixed herbs	1 teaspoon mixed herbs
50g/2oz mushrooms	½ cup mushrooms
1½ tablespoons tomato purée	1½ tablespoons tomato paste
salt and pepper	salt and pepper
75g/3oz Parmesan cheese, grated	¾ cup freshly grated Parmesan cheese
Garnish:	Garnish:
1 × 45g/1¾oz can anchovy fillets, drained	1 × 1¾oz can anchovy fillets, drained
black olives	ripe olives

1 Roll out the dough to fit a 25cm/10 inch plate.
2 Put the dough on a greased plate and leave in a warm place covered with a warm, damp tea (dish) towel until it has doubled in size (about 30 minutes).
3 Microwave risen dough on FULL POWER for 3½ minutes.
4 To prepare the filling: place bacon on a side plate and microwave on FULL POWER for 2 minutes. Drain off the fat.
5 Mix together the tomatoes, bacon, onion, herbs, mushrooms, tomato purée (paste) and salt and pepper.
6 Spread the filling over the risen dough and microwave on FULL POWER for 1½ minutes.
7 Sprinkle the cheese over the pizza and garnish with olives and anchovies. Microwave on FULL POWER for 2 minutes. Serve hot or cold.
Serves 4.
Total Microwave Cooking Time: 9 minutes

Risotto

METRIC/IMPERIAL	AMERICAN
225g/8oz long-grain rice	1 cup plus 2 tablespoons long-grain rice
600ml/1pt boiling water	2¼ cups boiling water
60g/2oz butter	4 tablespoons butter
salt and pepper	salt and pepper
100g/4oz frozen peas	1 cup frozen peas
4 gammon steaks (each weighing about 100g/4oz)	4 ham steaks (each weighing about ¼lb)
2 hard-boiled eggs, chopped	2 hard-cooked eggs, chopped
½ red pepper, deseeded and chopped	½ red pepper, deseeded and chopped

1 Place rice, boiling water, half the butter and salt into a 2.25 litre/4 pint (10 cup) mixing bowl, cover with plastic wrap and pierce.
2 Microwave on FULL POWER for 10 minutes.
3 Remove from microwave oven, stir and stand covered with a clean tea (dish) towel.
4 Place the peas in a small container. Add remaining butter, cover with plastic wrap and pierce. Microwave on FULL POWER for 2 minutes. Set aside.
5 Arrange bacon on 2 sheets kitchen paper in a circular fashion with fat side to the outside. Microwave on FULL POWER for 5 minutes turning steaks over once half way through cooking. Cool and chop.
6 Combine rice, chopped egg, peas, red pepper and bacon and serve.
Serves 4.
Total Microwave Cooking Time: 17 minutes

Cheese Omelette

METRIC/IMPERIAL	AMERICAN
1 tablespoon oil	1 tablespoon oil
2 large eggs	2 large eggs
2 tablespoons water	2 tablespoons water
salt and pepper	salt and pepper
50g/2oz cheese, grated	½ cup grated cheese

1 Preheat a deep browning dish: 3½ minutes on FULL POWER for the small size; 5 minutes on FULL POWER for the large size.
2 Pour the oil onto the heated dish and microwave on FULL POWER for 2 minutes.
3 Beat together the eggs and water, and season with salt and pepper
4 Pour the beaten eggs into the dish and microwave on FULL POWER for 1½ minutes.
5 Sprinkle grated cheese over the surface and fold the omelette in half.
6 Microwave on FULL POWER for 30 seconds.
Serves 1.
Total Microwave Cooking Time: 2½ minutes

Macaroni Cheese

METRIC/IMPERIAL	AMERICAN
1 small onion, peeled and chopped	1 small onion, peeled and chopped
½ red pepper, seeded and chopped	½ red pepper, seeded and chopped
225g/8oz quick cooking macaroni	2 cups quick cooking macaroni
900ml/1½ pints boiling chicken stock (boil a kettle and use 2 chicken stock cubes)	3¾ cups boiling chicken bouillon (boil a kettle and use 4 chicken bouillon cubes)
2 tablespoons cornflour	2 tablespoons cornstarch
150g/5oz Cheddar cheese, finely grated	1¼ cups finely grated Cheddar cheese
100g/4oz luncheon meat cut into cubes, or 100g/4oz cooked chicken, chopped	1 cup cubed luncheon meat, or 1 cup cooked, chopped chicken
Toasted Crumbs (see page 59)	Toasted Crumbs (see page 59)
Garnish:	Garnish:
tomato slices	tomato slices
chopped parsley	chopped parsley

1 Put the onion and pepper into a small dish. Cover with plastic wrap, and pierce.
2 Microwave on FULL POWER for 1½ minutes. Set aside.
3 Put the macaroni into a 2.25 litre/4 pint (10 cup) mixing bowl. Pour on boiling stock (bouillon).
4 Cover with plastic wrap, and pierce. Microwave on FULL POWER for 8 minutes. Allow to stand, covered, for 5 minutes.
5 Blend the cornflour (cornstarch) with a little cold water, and stir into the cooked macaroni together with 100g/¼lb (1 cup) of the cheese.
6 Stir in the luncheon meat or chicken, the softened onion and red pepper. Pour into a serving dish. Sprinkle with Toasted Crumbs, mixed with remaining cheese.
7 Microwave on POWER 7 for 3 minutes. Garnish with tomato slices and parsley before serving.
Serves 4.
Total Microwave Cooking Time: 12½ minutes

Family Scrambled Eggs

METRIC/IMPERIAL	AMERICAN
4 large eggs	4 large eggs
150ml/¼ pint milk	⅔ cup milk
25g/1oz butter	2 tablespoons butter
salt and pepper	salt and pepper
hot, buttered toast	hot, buttered toast

1 Beat together eggs and milk in a 1.75 litre/3 pint (7½ cup) mixing bowl. Add the butter and season well with salt and pepper.
2 Microwave uncovered on FULL POWER for 3–4 minutes until well risen and almost set.
3 Beat well with a balloon whisk.
4 Serve piled onto hot, buttered toast.
Serves 2.
Total Microwave Cooking Time: 3 minutes

Risotto; Family Scrambled Eggs

Microwave Bacon

Bacon can be cooked either on absorbent kitchen paper, a browning dish, or on a special Microwave bacon rack.

Method One:
1 Lay the bacon slices on a double thickness of kitchen paper, on a dinner plate. Leave a space in the centre and keep fatty parts of bacon to outside edge.
2 Microwave on FULL POWER for about 1 minute for each slice. Leave to stand for 2 minutes during which time the bacon will crisp and colour.

Method Two:
1 Preheat a browning dish: 3 minutes on FULL POWER for the small size; 5 minutes on FULL POWER for the large size.
2 Lay the bacon on the hot dish. DO NOT COVER.
3 Microwave on FULL POWER for about 1 minute for each slice, turning bacon over half-way through cooking.

Method Three:
1 Lay the bacon slices on the microwave bacon rack.
2 Microwave on FULL POWER for about 1 minute for each slice. The fat will drain away and the bacon will crisp.

Toasted Crumbs

This recipe is needed for many savoury dishes. The crumbs keep well and can be prepared in bulk and frozen or refrigerated in an airtight container.

METRIC/IMPERIAL	AMERICAN
100g/4oz fresh white or brown breadcrumbs	**2 cups fresh white or brown breadcrumbs**
50g/2oz butter	**¼ cup butter**

1 Put the butter in a 1 litre/1¾ pint (4¼ cup) jug and Microwave on FULL POWER for 1½ minutes.
2 Stir in the breadcrumbs and coat with the butter.
3 Microwave on FULL POWER for 2 minutes. Stir well, breaking down any lumps.
4 Microwave on FULL POWER for 2 minutes. Stir. Microwave on FULL POWER for 1½ minutes. Stir and set aside.
5 During a brief standing time crumbs will crisp up. Cool completely before storing.
Total Microwave Cooking Time: 7 minutes

Puddings & Desserts

Puddings and desserts can be cooked so quickly
in a microwave oven that a hostess can offer a choice of two
or three very different dishes, all of which
can be made in the time it normally takes to cook one.

Apricot Compôte

METRIC/IMPERIAL	AMERICAN
250g/9oz dried apricots	1½ cups dried apricots
1 pint boiling water	2½ cups boiling water
1 slice fresh lemon	1 slice fresh lemon
75g/3oz caster sugar	6 tablespoons sugar, firmly packed
25g/1oz raisins	3 tablespoons raisins
50g/2oz flaked almonds, toasted (optional)	½ cup flaked almonds, toasted (optional)
whipped cream to decorate	whipped cream to decorate

1 Place the apricots in a 1.2 litre/2 pint (5 cup) mixing bowl, and pour over the boiling water.
2 Add the lemon and sugar and stir well.
3 Cover with plastic wrap, and pierce. Microwave on FULL POWER for 12 minutes stirring once after 6 minutes.
4 Stir in the raisins, then allow to cool completely. If possible, chill overnight.
5 Sprinkle with toasted almonds if using and serve with whipped cream.
Serves 4.
Total Microwave Cooking Time: 6 minutes

Summer Fruit Mousse

METRIC/IMPERIAL	AMERICAN
500g/1lb mixed summer fruits, such as blackcurrants, strawberries and raspberries, hulled	1lb mixed summer fruits, such as blackcurrants, strawberries and raspberries, hulled
1 tablespoon water	1 tablespoon water
100g/4oz caster sugar	½ cup superfine sugar, firmly packed
1 envelope or 3 teaspoons gelatine dissolved in 7 tablespoons warm water	3 teaspoons gelatin dissolved in 7 tablespoons warm water
150ml/¼ pint whipping cream	⅔ cup heavy cream
2 egg whites	2 egg whites
whipped cream to decorate (optional)	whipped cream to decorate (optional)

1 Layer the fruit in a 2.25 litre/4 pint (10 cup) casserole.
2 Add the water and cover with a lid or plastic wrap, pierced. Microwave on FULL POWER for 5 minutes, and immediately stir in the sugar so that it dissolves.
3 Sieve the fruit and fold in the prepared gelatine. Cover and set aside in a refrigerator for 40 minutes.
4 Half whip the cream and fold it into the fruit mixture. Whip the egg whites in a clean bowl until they stand in peaks. Fold into the fruit mixture, using a metal spoon.
5 Pour into sundae dishes and chill to set. Decorate with whipped cream, if required.
Serves 3–4.
Total Microwave Cooking Time: 5 minutes

Summer Fruit Mousse; Apricot Compôte; Rice Pudding

Rice Pudding

METRIC/IMPERIAL	AMERICAN
50g/2oz short-grain rice	4 tablespoons short-grain rice
600ml/1 pint milk	2½ cups milk
25g/1oz sugar	2 tablespoons sugar
25g/1oz butter, flaked	2 tablespoons butter, flaked
2 tablespoons single cream or top-of-the milk	2 tablespoons half-and-half
a little grated nutmeg	a little grated nutmeg

1 Put the rice, milk and sugar in a 2 litre/3–4 pint (4–5 pint) mixing bowl, and stir well. Put the butter on the top.
2 Cover with plastic wrap and pierce. Microwave on FULL POWER for 4 minutes, then stir.
3 Microwave on POWER 7 for 20 minutes, stirring once. Stand for 5 minutes.
4 Stir in the cream and sprinkle with grated nutmeg.
Serves 3–4.
Total Microwave Cooking Time: 24 minutes

Caramelized Oranges

METRIC/IMPERIAL	AMERICAN
4 large oranges	4 large oranges
1 tablespoon Grand Marnier or kirsch	1 tablespoon Grand Marnier or kirsch
175g/6oz caster sugar	¾ cup sugar, firmly packed
120ml/4fl oz cold water	½ cup cold water
Yogurt or whipped cream to serve	yogurt or whipped cream to serve

1 Peel one orange, very thinly, taking care not to remove any pith.
2 Cut the peel into very fine strips and retain.
3 Peel the remaining oranges, removing all the pith, and remove the pith from the first orange.
4 Slice the oranges, removing any pips (seeds).
5 Arrange the slices in a 30 × 20 × 5cm/12 × 8 × 2 inch ovenproof glass dish. Spoon the liqueur over the slices, and add the orange peel.
6 Place the sugar and water in a 1 litre/1¾ pint (4½ cup) jug and microwave on FULL POWER for 10–13 minutes, until a dark golden caramel results.
7 Pour the caramel over the oranges.
8 Cool the oranges, then chill overnight in the refrigerator. Serve with yogurt or whipped cream.
Serves 4.
Total Microwave Cooking Time: 10 minutes

Family Apple Amber

METRIC/IMPERIAL	AMERICAN
100g/4oz butter	½ cup butter
100g/4oz fresh white or brown breadcrumbs mixed with 100g/4oz rolled oats	2 cups fresh white or brown breadcrumbs mixed with 1 cup rolled oats
or 225g/8oz breadcrumbs	or 4 cups breadcrumbs
1kg/2lb apples (a mixture of cookers and eaters), peeled and cored	2lb apples (a mixture of baking and eating), peeled and cored
50g/2oz caster sugar	¼ cup sugar, firmly packed
a few raisins	a few raisins
75g/3oz demerara sugar	½ cup light brown sugar
2 teaspoons mixed spice	2 teaspoons apple pie spice
50g/2oz chopped walnuts (optional)	½ cup chopped walnuts (optional)
cream or Custard Sauce to serve (see page 73)	cream or Custard Sauce to serve (see page 73)

1 Place butter in 1.75 litre/3 pint (7½ cup) mixing bowl and Microwave on FULL POWER for 1½ minutes.
2 Stir in the breadcrumbs, and oats if used. Coat with the butter.
3 Microwave on FULL POWER for 3 minutes. Stir well.
4 Microwave on FULL POWER for 2 minutes. Stir well.
5 Slice the apples into a 19cm/7½ inch deep soufflé dish or casserole and layer with white sugar and raisins.
6 Add the demerara (brown) sugar, spice and nuts (if used) to the breadcrumb mixture.
7 Sprinkle crumble over prepared fruit.
8 Microwave, uncovered, on FULL POWER for 5 minutes.
9 Allow to stand for 3 minutes. Serve with cream or Custard Sauce.
Serves 4–6.
Total Microwave Cooking Time: 11½ minutes

Caramelized Oranges; Family Apple Amber; Golden Baked Apples

Golden Baked Apples

METRIC/IMPERIAL	AMERICAN
4 large Bramley apples	4 large baking apples
4 teaspoons mincemeat	4 teaspoons mincemeat
½ teaspoon mixed spice	½ teaspoon apple pie spice
4 tablespoons golden syrup or thin honey	4 tablespoons light corn syrup or thin honey
4 tablespoons pure orange juice	4 tablespoons pure orange juice
glacé cherries or a few toasted almonds to decorate (optional)	candied cherries or a few toasted almonds to decorate (optional)

1 Core the apples and then use a small piece of each core to file the base of each apple.
2 Half-way down each apple make a very shallow cut all the way round.
3 Mix the mincemeat with the spice and use to fill each apple cavity.
4 Place the apples in a shallow dish. Pour the dessertspoon of syrup or honey over each one.
5 Pour the orange juice into the base of a 30 × 20 × 5cm/ 12 × 8 × 2 inch ovenproof glass dish. Cover with plastic wrap, and pierce.
6 Microwave on FULL POWER for 7–10 minutes. Stand for 3 minutes.
7 Spoon the orange juice over the apples. Decorate with glacé (candied) cherries or a few toasted almonds if liked and serve with vanilla ice cream.
Serves 4.
Total Microwave Cooking Time: 7 minutes

Topsy Turvy Cherry Pudding

METRIC/IMPERIAL	AMERICAN
1 × 400g/14oz can cherry pie filling	1 × 14oz can cherry pie filling
1 packet chocolate sponge cake mix	1 package chocolate sponge cake mix
eggs, as directed by packet instructions	eggs, as directed by package instructions
custard or cream to serve	custard or cream to serve

1 Spread the pie filling over the base of a 19cm/7½ inch soufflé dish, 10cm/4 inches deep.
2 Make up the cake mix according to directions, adding the eggs and 1 tablespoon of water.
3 Spread the sponge mixture evenly over the pie filling.
4 Microwave on FULL POWER for 5½ minutes.
5 Remove from microwave oven, cover with a dinner plate, and stand for 2 minutes.
6 Turn out onto a plate and serve with custard or cream.
Serves 6.
Total Microwave Cooking Time: 5½ minutes

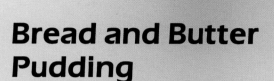

Bread and Butter Pudding

METRIC/IMPERIAL	AMERICAN
25g/1oz soft butter	2 tablespoons soft butter
12 thin slices white bread with crusts removed, well buttered and cut into quarters	12 thin slices white bread with crusts removed, well buttered and cut into quarters
100g/4oz seedless raisins	1 cup seedless raisins
½ teaspoon mixed spice	½ teaspoon apple pie spice
1½ tablespoons soft brown sugar	1½ tablespoons light brown sugar
Egg Custard:	Egg Custard:
4 eggs	4 eggs
600ml/1 pint milk	2½ cups milk
4 tablespoons caster sugar	4 tablespoons sugar
½ teaspoon vanilla essence	½ teaspoon vanilla
50g/2oz demerara sugar	⅓ cup light brown sugar

Lemon Sorbet;
Microwave Trifle;
Bread and Butter Pudding

1 Use the soft butter to grease the base and sides of a 30 × 20 × 5cm/12 × 8 × 2 inch ovenproof glass dish.
2 Cover the base of the dish with a layer of the bread, buttered side up.
3 Sprinkle with half the raisins, half the spice and half the brown sugar.
4 Add a second layer of bread and spinkle on the remaining raisins, spice and brown sugar.
5 Top with a final layer of bread, buttered side up.
6 To make the egg custard: beat the eggs in a 1.75 litre/3 pint (7½ cup) jug.
7 Put the milk, sugar and vanilla in a 1 litre/1¾ pint (4½ cup) jug and microwave on FULL POWER for 3½ minutes.
8 Pour the hot milk mixture onto the eggs, beating well with a rotary whisk.
9 Strain the mixture onto the bread and leave to stand for 15 minutes to allow the bread to absorb most of the liquid. Do not cover.
10 Microwave on POWER 5 for 12–15 minutes. Allow to stand for 5 minutes until set.
11 Before serving sprinkle with the brown sugar and, if liked, place under a preheated hot grill (broiler) to crisp the top.
Serves 6–8.
Total Microwave Cooking Time: 15½ minutes

Microwave Trifle

METRIC/IMPERIAL	AMERICAN
1 packet sponge mix – made up as directed but add 2 extra tablespoons milk	1 package sponge mix – made up as directed but add 2 extra tablespoons milk
1 tablespoon caster sugar	1 tablespoon sugar
cherry jam (about 2 tablespoons)	cherry jam (about 2 tablespoons)
1 recipe Apricot Compôte (see page 61), refrigerated overnight	1 recipe Apricot Compôte (see page 61), refrigerated overnight
4 tablespoons sherry	4 tablespoons sherry
few drops of almond essence	few drops of almond extract
1 recipe Custard Sauce (see page 73)	1 recipe Custard Sauce (see page 73)
1 egg yolk	1 egg yolk
300ml/½ pint whipping cream	1¼ cups whipping cream
Decoration:	Decoration:
angelica	angelica
glacé cherries	candied cherries

1 To cook the sponge: first prepare a 19cm/7½ inch soufflé dish by lightly brushing base and sides with oil. Put a circle of greaseproof in the base and coat sides with sugar. Knock out any surplus sugar.
2 Put prepared mixture into the soufflé dish and microwave on FULL POWER for 4 minutes.
3 Allow to stand, covered, for 4 minutes before turning out onto a cooling rack.
4 Split the cooled sponge cake in half and spread with jam. Sandwich together and cut into chunks.
5 Use sponge chunks to line a large deep glass serving dish.
6 Drain the juice from the apricots and mix with the sherry. Spoon over the sponge and press down with the back of a metal spoon.
7 Mix the apricots with the almond essence (extract) and pile evenly on to the sponge.
8 Cool the custard sauce slightly and beat in the egg yolk.
9 Pour the custard over the apricots to cover. Cool and refrigerate to set.
10 Whisk the cream until it stands in soft peaks, then spread over the custard to cover.
11 Using a fork, make a pattern on the cream and decorate with glacé (candied) cherries and angelica.
Serves 6.
Total Microwave Cooking Time: 10 minutes

Lemon Sorbet

METRIC/IMPERIAL	AMERICAN
3 large lemons, washed	3 large lemons, washed
225g/8oz caster sugar	1 cup sugar, firmly packed
600ml/1 pint water	2½ cups water
1 egg white	1 egg white
Optional Decoration:	Optional Decoration:
mint sprigs	mint sprigs
finely grated lemon rind	finely grated lemon rind

1 Set the refrigerator to its coldest setting.
2 Place the lemons on a dinner plate and microwave on FULL POWER for 1 minute. (This will improve the juice yield.)
3 Grate the rind from 2 lemons, very finely, avoiding any pith.
4 Squeeze the juice from the fruit and strain into a 2.25 litre/4 pint (10 cup) mixing bowl.
5 Put the sugar and water into a very large bowl (see Note). Stir, then microwave on FULL POWER for 4 minutes. Stir once during cooking. Stir again to ensure that sugar has dissolved.
6 Add the grated lemon rind. Cover with plastic wrap and pierce. Microwave on FULL POWER until boiling point is reached, about 4 minutes.
7 Stir and return to microwave oven, cook on FULL POWER for 8 minutes.
8 Strain the boiled syrup very carefully into the lemon juice.
9 Pour the mixture into ice trays and cool.
10 When cold freeze until mushy. This will take about 1 hour.
10 Turn into a large cold bowl, and beat until the mixture is almost white.
11 Quickly beat the egg white to soft peak stage. Fold into the sorbet, using a metal spoon.
12 Freeze until firm (3–4 hours).
13 Before serving, the sorbet should be placed in the main part of the refrigerator for about 1 hour so that the true flavour is realised. Serve decorated with a mint sprig and a little grated lemon rind.
Serves 4.
Total Microwave Cooking Time: 17 minutes

Note: the bowl will become very hot when the sugar syrup is boiled, so be sure to use oven gloves when removing it from the microwave oven.

Butterscotch Bananas

METRIC/IMPERIAL	AMERICAN
15g/½oz butter	1 tablespoon butter
25g/1oz soft brown sugar	2 tablespoons light brown sugar
1 tablespoon golden syrup	1 tablespoon light corn syrup
300ml/½ pint milk	1¼ cups milk
3 teaspoons cornflour	3 teaspoons cornstarch
3 medium-sized bananas	3 medium-sized bananas
juice of half a lemon (optional)	juice of half a lemon (optional)
40g/1½oz walnuts, roughly chopped or 40g/1½oz grated chocolate to decorate	½ cup roughly chopped walnuts or 1½oz grated chocolate to decorate

1 To make the sauce: put the butter, sugar and syrup into a 600ml/1 pint (2½ cup) ovenproof glass jug, and microwave on FULL POWER for 1 minute.
2 Stir and microwave on FULL POWER for 1½ minutes.
3 Stir in the milk, reserving 1 tablespoonful. Microwave on FULL POWER for 2½ minutes.
4 Cream the cornflour (cornstarch) with the remaining milk. Pour heated liquid onto mixed cornflour (cornstarch) and beat well.
5 Microwave on FULL POWER for 1 minute, or until boiling. Beat well with a balloon whisk.
6 Slice the bananas, arrange them in a dish and sprinkle with lemon juice if used.
7 Pour the sauce over to coat and microwave on FULL POWER for 1½ minutes.
8 Serve immediately, sprinkled with nuts or chocolate.
Serves 4.
Total Microwave Cooking Time: 7½ minutes

Note: When the cold milk is added the caramel will harden, but as the milk warms it will melt again and blend into the sauce to give the butterscotch flavour.

Cornerways Crumble

METRIC/IMPERIAL	AMERICAN
75g/3oz butter	6 tablespoons butter
225g/8oz muesli	½lb Swiss muesli
750g/1½lb rhubarb, sliced	1½lb rhubarb, sliced
50g/2oz caster sugar	¼ cup sugar, firmly packed
grated rind of 1 orange	grated rind of 1 orange
1 tablespoon orange juice	1 tablespoon orange juice
orange slices to decorate	orange slices to decorate

1 Place the butter in a 1 litre/1¾ pint (4½ cup) jug and microwave on FULL POWER for 1 minute.
2 Stir in the muesli. Mix well to coat with butter.
3 Layer the rhubarb with sugar, orange rind and orange juice in a 1.75 litre/3 pint (7½ cup) ovenproof glass casserole dish.
4 Sprinkle the muesli mix on top. DO NOT COVER.
5 Microwave, uncovered, on FULL POWER for 7–10 minutes.
6 Stand 3 minutes before serving hot with fresh cream. Alternatively, serve cold, decorated with slices of fresh oranges.
Serves 4.
Total Microwave Cooking Time: 6 minutes

Apple and Blackberry Snow

METRIC/IMPERIAL	AMERICAN
500g/1lb Bramley apples, peeled and thinly sliced	1lb baking apples, peeled and thinly sliced
225g/8oz fresh blackberries	2 cups fresh blackberries
75g/3oz caster sugar	6 tablespoons sugar, firmly packed
2 egg whites	2 egg whites

1 Put the apples and blackberries into a 1.2 litre/2 pint (5 cup) mixing bowl. Cover tightly with plastic wrap, and pierce.
2 Microwave on FULL POWER for 6½ minutes, stirring once, half-way through cooking. Allow to stand for 2 minutes.
3 Beat in the sugar.
4 Pass through a sieve into a 1.75 litre/3 pint (7½ cup) mixing bowl, and leave to cool.
5 Beat the egg whites in a clean bowl with a clean whisk until they stand in soft peaks.
6 Using a metal tablespoon, fold the egg whites into the fruit mixture.
7 Pile into sundae glasses, and chill.
Serves 4.
Total Microwave Cooking Time: 6½ minutes

Jam-Capped Suet Pudding

METRIC/IMPERIAL	AMERICAN
oil for greasing	oil for greasing
3 tablespoons raspberry jam	3 tablespoons raspberry jam
175g/6oz self-raising flour	1½ cups self-rising flour
75g/3oz caster sugar	6 tablespoons sugar
75g/3oz shredded suet	9 tablespoons shredded suet
2 large eggs	2 large eggs
5 tablespoons milk	⅓ cup milk

1 Lightly brush a 900ml/1½ pint (3¾ cup) pudding basin (slope-sided mold) with a little oil.
2 Spread the jam over the base and sides of pudding basin (mold).
3 Sift the flour into a 1.75 litre/3 pint (7½ cup) mixing bowl. Mix in the sugar and suet.
4 Beat together the eggs and milk and stir into the dry ingredients. Mix to combine.
5 Pile into the prepared pudding basin (mold) and level the top.
6 Microwave on POWER 4 for 12 minutes, giving the dish a half-turn, twice, during cooking. The top should still be just moist.
7 Allow to stand, covered, for 6 minutes before turning out. Serve with Custard Sauce (page 73).
Serves 6.
Total Microwave Cooking Time: 12 minutes

Apple and Blackberry Snow; Jam-Capped Suet Pudding; Cornerways Crumble

Chocolate Sauce

METRIC/IMPERIAL	AMERICAN
100g/4oz milk or plain chocolate, broken into squares	¼lb semi-sweet chocolate, broken into squares
25g/1oz butter	2 tablespoons butter
150ml/¼ pint water or milk	⅔ cup water or milk
1½ teaspoons cornflour	1½ teaspoons cornstarch

1 Put the chocolate, butter and water or milk into a 1 litre/ 1¾ pint (4½ cup) jug and microwave on POWER 7 for 3½ minutes.

2 Put the cornflour (cornstarch) in a 1.2 litre/2pint (5 cup) bowl and mix to a smooth paste with a little water.

3 Pour the hot chocolate mixture onto the cornflour (cornstarch), stirring all the time.

4 Return to the microwave on FULL POWER for 1 minute before serving. The sauce can be served hot or cold over fruit, sponge puddings or ice cream.

Serves 4.

Total Microwave Cooking Time: 4½ minutes

Rich Chocolate Pudding

METRIC/IMPERIAL	AMERICAN
2 large eggs	2 large eggs
50g/2oz caster sugar	¼ cup superfine sugar, firmly packed
25g/1oz plain flour	¼ cup all-purpose flour
25g/1oz cocoa	¼ cup unsweetened cocoa
hot Chocolate Sauce (opposite) to serve	hot Chocolate Sauce (opposite) to serve

1 Beat the eggs and sugar together in a 1.75 litre/3 pint (7½ cup) mixing bowl until thick and pale (about 4 minutes). Use an electric whisk or rotary beater.
2 Put the sieved flour and cocoa on a dinner plate and microwave on FULL POWER for 5 seconds.
3 Using a metal tablespoon, lightly fold the warmed cocoa and flour into the egg mixture.
4 Pour into an ungreased 1.2 litre/2 pint (5 cup) ovenproof glass pudding basin (slope-sided mold).
5 Microwave on FULL POWER for 3½ minutes.
6 Allow to stand for 3 minutes before turning out.
7 Serve with hot chocolate sauce.
Serves 4.
Total Microwave Cooking Time: 3½ minutes

Rich Chocolate Pudding with Chocolate Sauce; Chocolate Upside-Down Pudding; Vanilla Ice Cream with Chocolate Sauce (see page 73)

Chocolate Upside-Down Pudding

METRIC/IMPERIAL	AMERICAN
oil for greasing	oil for greasing
caster sugar for coating	sugar for coating
1 × 225g/8oz can pineapple slices, drained	1 × ½lb can pineapple slices, drained
5 glacé cherries, halved	5 candied cherries, halved
200g/7oz self-raising flour	1¾ cups self-rising flour
3 tablespoons drinking chocolate	3 tablespoons sweetened cocoa
100g/4oz soft margarine	½ cup soft margarine
100g/4oz caster sugar	½ cup sugar, firmly packed
100g/4oz soft dark brown sugar	⅔ cup light brown sugar
2 eggs, beaten	2 eggs, beaten
5 tablespoons evaporated milk, mixed with 5 tablespoons water	⅓ cup evaporated milk, mixed with ⅓ cup water

1 Prepare a 19cm/7½ inch soufflé dish. Lightly brush base and sides with oil. Fit a circle of greaseproof paper (non-stick parchment) in the base and use a little sugar to coat the sides. Knock out any surplus.
2 Arrange the pineapple and cherries in an attractive pattern on the base of the dish.
3 Sift together the flour, a little salt and drinking chocolate (sweetened cocoa) into a bowl.
4 Rub in the margarine until mixture resembles fine breadcrumbs; then stir in the sugars.
5 Make a well in the centre of the dry ingredients and, using an electric whisk, beat in the eggs then the milk and water mixture. Beat well for 1 minute.
6 Pour the mixture onto the pineapple and cherries and level the surface.
7 Microwave on FULL POWER for 10½–11 minutes, giving the dish a half-turn, three times during cooking, if necessary. The cake is cooked when a wooden cocktail stick (toothpick) inserted into the centre comes out clean.
8 Let the pudding stand, covered, for 5 minutes, before turning out. This pudding is delicious hot or cold.
Serves 6.
Total Microwave Cooking Time: 10½–11 minutes

Note: As a speedy alternative, a good quality packet sponge mix can be used instead of the recipe given here. Make up as directed on the packet, but add 2 extra tablespoons of water. Microwave on FULL POWER for 5 minutes.

Peachy Cheese Cake

METRIC/IMPERIAL
75g/3oz butter
175g/6oz digestive biscuits, crushed
100g/4oz caster sugar
3 tablespoons raspberry jam
1 × 415g/14½oz can sliced peaches, drained
225g/8oz cream cheese
150ml/¼ pint soured cream
2 eggs, separated
½ teaspoon almond essence
3 teaspoons cornflour, mixed with a little water
toasted almonds to decorate

AMERICAN
6 tablespoons butter
1½ cups crushed Graham crackers
8 tablespoons sugar
3 tablespoons raspberry jam
1 × 14½oz can sliced peaches, drained
1 cup cream cheese
⅔ cup sour cream
2 eggs, separated
½ teaspoon almond extract
3 teaspoons cornstarch, mixed with a little water
toasted almonds to decorate

1 Place the butter in a large mixing bowl and microwave on FULL POWER for 1½ minutes.
2 Mix in the biscuit (cracker) crumbs with 25g/1oz (2 tablespoons) sugar. Press over the base of a large soufflé dish or a 25cm/10 inch flan dish.
3 To make the jam easy to spread, place in a small dish and microwave on FULL POWER for a few seconds. Spread over the biscuit (cracker) base.
4 Chop the peaches, reserving 6 slices for decoration and arrange on the crust and refrigerate.
5 Place cream cheese in a large glass mixing bowl and microwave on POWER 5 for 2 minutes.
6 Beat in the remaining sugar, soured cream, egg yolks, almond essence (extract) and cornflour (cornstarch). Beat well.
7 Whip the egg whites until stiff and fold into the cheese mixture. Pour over the peaches to cover evenly.
8 Microwave on POWER 5 for 10 minutes. Give the dish a half-turn. Microwave on FULL POWER for 2 minutes.
9 Leave until quite cold. Decorate with reserved, drained peach slices and a few toasted almonds.
Serves 8.
Total Microwave Cooking Time: 15½ minutes

Rich Chocolate Mousse

METRIC/IMPERIAL	AMERICAN
225g/8oz milk or plain chocolate, broken into pieces	½lb semi-sweet chocolate, broken into pieces
4 large eggs, separated	4 large eggs, separated
Decoration:	Decoration:
150ml/¼ pint whipping cream	⅔ cup heavy cream
toasted almonds (see below)	toasted almonds (see below)

1 Place the chocolate in a 1.75 litre/3 pint (7½ cup) mixing bowl and microwave on POWER 4 for 7–8 minutes, until chocolate has melted. Stir twice during this time. Allow to cool for 5 minutes.
2 Beat the yolks, one at a time, into the chocolate.
3 Whisk the egg whites until they stand in soft peaks. Fold into the chocolate mixture, using a metal spoon.
4 Divide the mixture between four sundae dishes and refrigerate until set (about 1 hour).
5 Decorate with whipped cream and toasted nuts.
Serves 4.
Total Microwave Cooking Time: 8 minutes

Note: To toast nuts, place two sheets kitchen paper on a dinner plate and arrange about 25g/1oz flaked almonds in a ring around the edge. Microwave on FULL POWER for 1 minute. Rearrange nuts and microwave on FULL POWER for 1 minute. Cool completely before using.

Pineapple Delights

METRIC/IMPERIAL	AMERICAN
4 pineapple rings	4 pineapple rings
175g/6oz fresh raspberries	1 cup fresh raspberries
3 large egg whites	3 large egg whites
175g/6oz caster sugar	⅔ cup sugar, firmly packed
50g/2oz ground almonds	½ cup ground almonds

1 Put 1 pineapple ring in each of four fairly deep sundae dishes.
2 Divide the raspberries equally between the dishes.
3 To make the meringue: place the egg whites in a large grease-free bowl, and beat them until they are very stiff.
4 Beat in the sugar, 1 tablespoon at a time, and continue beating until all the sugar has been incorporated. The mixture will be very thick.
5 Using a metal spoon, fold in the ground almonds.
6 Stand each sundae dish on a tea plate and divide the meringue mixture between the four dishes.
7 Microwave all four together on FULL POWER for 3 minutes. Serve at once.
Serves 4.
Total Microwave Cooking Time: 3 minutes

Note: For a crisp brown top, finish this dessert by putting the sundae dishes under a preheated very hot grill (broiler). They will colour in a few seconds.

Rich Chocolate Mousse; Peachy Cheese Cake; Pineapple Delights

Fruity Apple Pudding

METRIC/IMPERIAL	AMERICAN
1 small egg	1 small egg
150ml/¼ pint milk	⅔ cup milk
1 large cooking apple, peeled, cored and grated	1 large baking apple, peeled, cored and grated
100g/4oz fresh breadcrumbs (brown or white)	2 cups fresh breadcrumbs (brown or white)
50g/2oz shredded suet	6 tablespoons shredded suet
175g/6oz dried mixed fruit	1 cup dried mixed fruit
1 tablespoon honey	1 tablespoon honey
1 teaspoon mixed spice	1 teaspoon apple pie spice
grated rind and juice of 1 orange	grated rind and juice of 1 orange
Honey Apple Sauce to serve	Honey Apple Sauce to serve

1 Beat together the egg and the milk.
2 Add all the remaining ingredients and mix well.
3 Pour into an ungreased 900ml/1½ pint (3¾ cup) mixing bowl. Cover with plastic wrap, and pierce.
4 Microwave on POWER 4 for 7 minutes. Then FULL POWER for 2 minutes.
5 Leave to stand while making Honey Apple Sauce (see right).
6 Turn the pudding onto a plate and pour over the hot sauce.
Serves 6.
Total Microwave Cooking Time: 9 minutes

Honey Apple Sauce

METRIC/IMPERIAL	AMERICAN
1½ teaspoons cornflour	1½ teaspoons cornstarch
150ml/¼ pint apple juice plus a few drops of lemon juice	⅔ cup apple juice plus a few drops of lemon juice
1 tablespoon runny honey	1 tablespoon runny honey
25g/1oz raisins	3 tablespoons raisins

1 Blend the cornflour (cornstarch) with a little apple juice to a smooth consistency.
2 Place the remaining apple juice, honey and raisins in a 1 litre/1¾ pint (4½ cup) jug and microwave on FULL POWER for 2 minutes.
3 Whisk in the blended cornflour (cornstarch) and microwave on FULL POWER for 1 minute. Serve with Fruity Apple Pudding.
Makes 150ml/¼ pint (⅔ cup)
Total Microwave Cooking Time: 3 minutes

Fruity Apple Pudding with Honey Apple Sauce; Custard Sauce; Vanilla Ice Cream

Coffee or Vanilla Ice Cream

METRIC/IMPERIAL	AMERICAN
300ml/½ pint double cream	1¼ cups heavy cream
300ml/½ pint single cream	1¼ cups light cream
50g/2oz caster sugar	¼ cup sugar, firmly packed
1½ teaspoons coffee essence or a few drops of vanilla essence	1½ teaspoons coffee extract or a few drops of vanilla
4 egg yolks	4 egg yolks
3 teaspoons cornflour	3 teaspoons cornstarch

1 Whip the double (heavy) cream to very soft peak stage. Refrigerate to chill.
2 Put a 1.2 litre/2 pint (5 cup) plastic ice cream container in the freezer.
3 Put the single (light) cream into a 1 litre/1¾ pint (4½ cup) jug and microwave on FULL POWER for 3 minutes until boiling.
4 Meanwhile beat together the sugar, coffee or vanilla essence and egg yolks in a large bowl. Blend the cornflour (cornstarch) into egg yolk mixture.
5 Pour the heated cream onto the egg yolk mixture, beating well with a balloon whisk.
6 Microwave on FULL POWER for 1–2 minutes until boiling point is reached.
7 Remove from oven, then beat again. Allow to stand for 10 minutes.
8 Place the mixing bowl in a large bowl containing ice cubes. Leave, beating occasionally, until quite cold.
9 Beat the refrigerated whipped cream into the custard. Put the bowl into the freezer until the ice cream reaches setting point (about 35 minutes).
10 Beat well with an electric hand whisk or rotary whisk.
11 Put the mixture into the ice cream container and freeze until firm (about 2 hours).
12 Before serving, allow the ice cream to stand in the refrigerator for half an hour. Serve with chocolate sauce if liked (see page 68).
Serves 4–6.
Total Microwave Cooking Time: 5 minutes

Custard Sauce

METRIC/IMPERIAL	AMERICAN
2 rounded tablespoons custard powder	2 rounded tablespoons Bird's English Dessert Mix
600ml/1 pint of milk	2½ cups milk
2 tablespoons sugar	2 tablespoons sugar, firmly packed

1 Cream the custard powder with a little milk in a 900ml/1½ pint (3¾ cup) bowl.
2 Pour the remaining milk into a 1 litre/1¾ pint (4½ cup) jug and microwave on FULL POWER for 2 minutes.
3 Pour warmed milk onto mixed custard powder. Stir well and return to the jug.
4 Microwave on FULL POWER for 3–4 minutes. Beat in the sugar until it has dissolved.
5 Beat well with balloon whisk and serve.
Serves 6.
Total Microwave Cooking Time: 6 minutes

Christmas Pudding

METRIC/IMPERIAL	AMERICAN
175g/6oz plain flour	1½ cups all-purpose flour
150g/5oz fresh breadcrumbs (brown or white)	2½ cups fresh breadcrumbs (brown or white)
50g/2oz butter, grated (straight from the refrigerator)	¼ cup butter, grated (straight from the refrigerator)
100g/4oz shredded suet	¾ cup shredded suet
½ teaspoon salt	½ teaspoon salt
¾ teaspoon mixed spice	¾ teaspoon apple pie spice
1 small eating apple, peeled and grated	1 small eating apple, peeled and grated
100g/4oz soft brown sugar	⅔ cup light brown sugar
100g/4oz caster sugar	½ cup sugar, firmly packed
25g/1oz glacé cherries, washed and chopped	¼ cup candied cherries, washed and chopped
75g/3oz ground almonds	¾ cup ground almonds
750g/1½lb mixed dried fruit (sultanas, raisins, currants and peel)	4½ cups mixed dried fruit (golden raisins, raisins, currants and candied peel)
grated rind and juice of 1 orange	grated rind and juice of 1 orange
grated rind and juice of 1 lemon	grated rind and juice of 1 lemon
1 tablespoon black treacle	1 tablespoon molasses
4 tablespoons sherry	4 tablespoons sherry
4 teaspoons gravy browning	4 teaspoons gravy coloring
3 large eggs	3 large eggs
150ml/¼ pint of milk	⅔ cup of milk
extra caster sugar for dredging	extra sugar for dredging

1 Put the flour and breadcrumbs into a large mixing bowl.

2 Rub in the butter, then mix in the suet.

3 Add the salt, spice, apple, brown and white sugar, glacé (candied) cherries, ground almonds, dried fruit and the rind from the orange and the lemon. Mix well.

4 Mix together in a small bowl, the juice of the orange and lemon, the black treacle (molasses), sherry and gravy browning colouring.

5 Beat together the eggs and the milk in another bowl.

6 Stir the liquid ingredients, alternately, into the dry ingredients, mixing well until combined.

7 Divide the mixture between 2 × 900ml/1½ pint (3¾ cup) boilable plastic pudding basins (slope-sided ovenproof molds). Level the tops. Cover with plastic wrap, and pierce.

8 MICROWAVE EACH PUDDING SEPARATELY. Microwave on POWER 7 for 12 minutes, giving the dish a half-turn, twice during cooking, if necessary. Remove from microwave oven and allow to stand for 15 minutes, covered with foil, before turning out.

9 Dredge with white sugar and serve with brandy sauce (see opposite) or brandy butter.

Serves 6.

Total Microwave Cooking Time: 12 minutes for one pudding

To flame the pudding:
Put 2 tablespoons of brandy into a glass. Microwave on FULL POWER for 30 seconds. Pour over the pudding and light immediately.

To reheat 1 × 2lb Christmas pudding:
Cover with plastic wrap, and pierce. Microwave on FULL POWER for 3½ minutes, giving the pudding a half-turn, half-way through cooking. Allow to stand, covered, for 3 minutes before serving.

To reheat a slice of Christmas pudding:
Cover with plastic wrap, and pierce. Microwave on FULL POWER for 15–30 seconds. Allow to stand for 30 seconds.

Christmas Pudding; Brandy Sauce; Sherried Almond Pears

Sherried Almond Pears

METRIC/IMPERIAL	AMERICAN
2 large ripe pears, halved, peeled and cored	2 large ripe pears, halved, peeled and cored
50g/2oz butter	¼ cup butter
25g/1oz soft brown sugar	2 tablespoons light brown sugar
50g/2oz ground almonds (for economy use half cake crumbs, half ground almonds)	½ cup ground almonds (for economy use half almonds, half cake crumbs)
2 drops almond essence	2 drops almond extract
1 tablespoon sherry	1 tablespoon sherry
120ml/4fl oz white wine *or* pure orange juice	½ cup white wine *or* pure orange juice
2 glacé cherries, halved	2 candied cherries, halved
whipped cream to decorate	whipped cream to decorate

1 Arrange the pear halves, hollow part upwards, in an attractive shallow serving dish.
2 Place the butter in a large jug and microwave on POWER 2 for 2 minutes.
3 Beat in the sugar, ground almonds, almond essence (extract) and sherry, a little at a time. Use to fill the four hollows.
4 Pour wine or orange juice into the base of the dish. Cover with plastic wrap and pierce.
5 Microwave on FULL POWER for 2–3 minutes. (The length of time will depend on the size and ripeness of the pear halves.)
6 Spoon the wine or juice over the pears. Serve hot or cold, decorated with half a cherry and whipped cream.
Serves 2–4.
Total Microwave Cooking Time: 4–5 minutes

Variation
Canned or fresh peach halves can be used. Prepare and microwave as above.

Brandy Sauce

METRIC/IMPERIAL	AMERICAN
1½ tablespoons cornflour	1½ tablespoons cornstarch
300ml/½ pint milk	1¼ cups milk
25g/1oz caster sugar	2 tablespoons sugar, firmly packed
2 tablespoons brandy	2 tablespoons brandy
25g/1oz butter	2 tablespoons butter

1 In a 1.2 litre/2 pint (5 cup) mixing bowl, mix the cornflour (cornstarch) with a little milk, until a smooth paste results.
2 Put the remaining milk into a 1 litre/1¾ pint (4¼ cup) jug and microwave on FULL POWER for 1 minute.
3 Pour the heated milk onto the cornflour (cornstarch) mixture, stirring all the time.
4 Return to the jug and microwave on FULL POWER for 1–2 minutes, until boiling. Beat well with a balloon whisk.
5 Beat in the sugar, brandy and butter, and serve hot.
Serves 4.
Total Microwave Cooking Time: 3 minutes

Microwave Baking

Cakes expand like magic when cooking in a microwave oven
so always use a suitably large container.
A basic sponge cake will remain rather pale but it can be coloured
under a preheated grill (broiler) or masked with an
attractive topping. Some cakes may appear to have a slightly
damp surface even though they are cooked, they will
dry out during the standing time.

Strawberry Gâteau

METRIC/IMPERIAL	AMERICAN
oil for greasing	oil for greasing
175g/6oz caster sugar	¾ cup sugar, firmly packed
175g/6oz self-raising flour, sifted	1½ cups self-rising flour, sifted
175g/6oz soft margarine	¾ cup soft margarine
3 large eggs	3 large eggs
3 tablespoons milk	3 tablespoons milk
2 tablespoons strawberry jam	2 tablespoons strawberry jam
300ml/½ pint double cream, whipped and chilled	1¼ cups heavy cream, whipped and chilled
50g/2oz flaked almonds, toasted (see page 71)	½ cup flaked almonds, toasted (see page 71)
225g/½lb fresh strawberries	1½ cups fresh strawberries
strips of angelica to decorate	strips of angelica to decorate

1 Prepare a 19cm/7½ inch soufflé dish by lightly brushing sides and base with oil. Line the base with a circle of greaseproof paper (non-stick parchment). Coat the sides with a little extra sugar; knock out any surplus.
2 Put the sugar, flour, margarine, eggs and milk into a mixing bowl and beat until smooth. Continue beating for 2 minutes by hand or for 1 minute if using an electric mixer.
3 Pour the mixture into the soufflé dish.
4 Microwave on FULL POWER for about 7–9 minutes (giving the dish a half-turn, twice during cooking, if necessary), until a wooden cocktail stick (toothpick), inserted into the centre, comes out clean.
5 Allow to stand for 5 minutes before turning out onto a cooling rack which has been covered with a clean tea (dish) towel. Cool, and remove the paper.
6 When cold, cut the cake in half across the centre. Fill with the jam and sandwich the two halves together again.
7 Coat the sides of the cake with some of the whipped cream, then roll the sides in the nuts to coat.
8 Spread some of the remaining cream on the top to cover.
9 Decorate with strawberries, angelica and rosettes of cream.
Serves 6.
Total Microwave Cooking Time: 7–9 minutes

Chocolate Gâteau; Strawberry Gâteau

Chocolate Gâteau

METRIC/IMPERIAL	AMERICAN
oil or butter for greasing	oil or butter for greasing
3 large eggs	3 large eggs
2 tablespoons milk	2 tablespoons milk
1 tablespoon golden syrup	1 tablespoon light corn syrup
150g/5oz self-raising flour	1¼ cups self-rising flour
25g/1oz cocoa powder	¼ cup unsweetened cocoa
175g/6oz soft margarine	¾ cup soft margarine
175g/6oz caster sugar	¾ cup sugar, firmly packed
3 tablespoons lemon curd	3 tablespoons lemon curd
Decoration:	Decoration:
75g/3oz plain chocolate	3oz semi-sweet chocolate
150ml/¼ pint cream, whipped	⅔ cup heavy cream, whipped
chopped nuts (optional)	chopped nuts (optional)

1 Grease the base of a soufflé dish, 19cm/7½ inch in diameter, 10cm/4 inches deep. Cut a ring of greaseproof paper (non-stick parchment) and bottom line the dish. DO NOT apply more oil on the base or sides.
2 Put the eggs, milk, syrup, flour, cocoa, margarine and sugar in the bowl of an electric mixer. Mix to combine and then beat 1 minute on maximum. Alternatively, combine by hand and beat for 2 minutes with a wooden spoon.
3 Put all the mixture into the prepared soufflé dish and level the top.
4 Microwave on FULL POWER for 7–9 minutes, until a wooden cocktail stick (toothpick) inserted into the centre comes out clean.
5 Remove from microwave oven and stand for 5 minutes, covered with a clean tea (dish) towel.
6 Turn onto a cooling rack and, when cold, split and fill with lemon curd.
7 Melt the chocolate on POWER 3 for 4 minutes. Beat well until smooth.
8 Pour the melted chocolate over the cake.
9 Allow to cool. Decorate gâteau with rosettes of whipped cream and a scattering of nuts if liked.
Serves 6.
Total Microwave Cooking Time: 11–13 minutes

Lemon and Honey Crispies

METRIC/IMPERIAL	AMERICAN
100g/4oz margarine	½ cup margarine
50g/2oz caster sugar	¼ cup sugar, firmly packed
2 tablespoons runny honey or golden syrup	2 tablespoons runny honey or light corn syrup
2 teaspoons lemon juice	2 teaspoons lemon juice
25g/1oz raisins	3 tablespoons raisins
100g/4oz cornflakes	1 cup cornflakes
paper cake cases	paper cake cases
a little chocolate vermicelli or coloured sugar strands	a little chocolate vermicelli or multicolored sprinkles

1 Put the margarine, sugar and honey or syrup into a 1.75 litre/3 pint (7½ cup) glass mixing bowl.
2 Microwave on FULL POWER for 1 minute, and stir. Microwave on POWER 5 for 3 minutes.
3 Stir to ensure that the sugar is dissolved. Stir in the lemon juice, raisins and cornflakes.
4 Arrange the cake cases on a cooling tray and pile a small amount of Cornflakes mixture into each cake case. Leave to set.
5 Just before the crispies have set, sprinkle some chocolate vermicelli or coloured sugar strands on top of each.
Makes 20.
Total Microwave Cooking Time: 4 minutes

Walnut Biscuits (Cookies)

METRIC/IMPERIAL	AMERICAN
75g/3oz soft margarine	¼ cup plus 2 tablespoons soft margarine
50g/2oz soft brown sugar	⅓ cup light brown sugar
100g/4oz self-raising flour, sifted	1 cup self-rising flour, sifted
½ teaspoon mixed spice	½ teaspoon apple pie spice
½ egg, beaten	½ egg, beaten
12 walnut halves	12 walnut halves

1 Beat together the margarine and sugar until light and fluffy.
2 Using a metal spoon, fold in the flour and spice with the egg. Mix well.
3 Turn onto a lightly floured board and knead until smooth.
4 Roll into 12 even-sized balls and arrange 6 on an ungreased 30 × 20 × 5cm/12 × 8 × 2 inch ovenproof glass dish (three down each side).
5 Press half a walnut on top of each one, and microwave on POWER 7 for 4 minutes.
6 Remove from microwave oven and allow to cool slightly before transferring to cooling rack.
7 Repeat with remaining 6 biscuits (cookies).
Makes 12.
Total Microwave Cooking Time: 8 minutes

Note: These biscuits (cookies) will harden on cooling, store in an airtight tin.

Date Cake

METRIC/IMPERIAL	AMERICAN
oil for greasing	oil for greasing
a little caster sugar	a little superfine sugar
175g/6oz self-raising flour, sifted	1½ cups self-rising flour, sifted
½ teaspoon mixed spice	½ teaspoon apple pie spice
100g/4oz soft margarine	½ cup soft margarine
75g/3oz soft dark brown sugar	½ cup dark brown sugar
100g/4oz stoned chopped dates	⅔ cup stoned, chopped dates
2 large eggs	2 large eggs
4 tablespoons milk	4 tablespoons milk
1 tablespoon black treacle	1 tablespoon molasses
1 teaspoon gravy browning	1 teaspoon gravy coloring

1 Lightly brush a 19cm/7½ inch soufflé dish with oil and coat the base and sides with a sprinkling of sugar; knock out any surplus.
2 Sift the flour and spice into a mixing bowl and rub in the fat.
3 Add the sugar and dates, and mix well.
4 Beat together the eggs, milk, treacle (molasses) and gravy browning (coloring). Stir into the dry ingredients and mix well to combine.
5 Pour the cake mixture into the prepared dish. Level the top. Do not cover.
6 Microwave on FULL POWER for 5½ minutes, giving the dish a half-turn, half-way through cooking, if necessary.
7 Allow to stand, covered with a clean tea (dish) towel, for 6 minutes.
8 Turn out onto a cooling rack and allow to cool completely.
9 Before serving, sprinkle with a little caster (superfine) sugar.
Serves 8.
Total Microwave Cooking Time: 5½ minutes

Bread Pudding; Lemon and Honey Crispies; Date Cake; Walnut Biscuits (Cookies)

Bread Pudding

METRIC/IMPERIAL	AMERICAN
8 thick slices slightly stale bread, including crusts, cut into small pieces	8 thick slices slightly stale bread, including crusts, cut into small pieces
2 eggs, beaten	2 eggs, beaten
350ml/12fl oz milk	1½ cups milk
1 medium-sized, ripe banana, peeled, and sliced	1 medium-sized, ripe banana, peeled and sliced
350g/12oz mixed dried fruit (raisins, currants, sultanas, peel)	2 cups mixed dried fruit (raisins, currants, golden raisins, candied peel)
50g/2oz glacé cherries, washed and chopped	¼ cup candied cherries, washed and chopped
75g/3oz soft dark brown sugar	½ cup dark brown sugar
2 teaspoons gravy browning	2 teaspoons gravy coloring
1 tablespoon black treacle	1 tablespoon molasses
1 tablespoon apricot jam or marmalade	1 tablespoon apricot jam or marmalade
40g/1½oz self-raising flour	¼ cup plus 2 tablespoons self-rising flour
1 teaspoon lemon juice	1 teaspoon lemon juice
1 teaspoon ground cinnamon	1 teaspoon ground cinnamon
2 teaspoons mixed spice	2 teaspoons apple pie spice
50g/2oz butter, melted	¼ cup butter, melted
25g/1oz mixed nuts, chopped (optional)	¼ cup chopped, mixed nuts (optional)
a little caster sugar	a little superfine sugar

1 Place the bread pieces in a 2.25 litre/4 pint (10 cup) mixing bowl.
2 Beat together the eggs and milk. Pour over the bread and leave to soak for 20 minutes.
3 Beat well with a fork.
4 Add all the remaining ingredients and beat well with a wooden spoon to combine.
5 Divide between two 1kg/2lb plastic loaf containers. Cover with plastic wrap, and pierce.
6 MICROWAVE EACH CONTAINER SEPARATELY. Microwave on POWER 7 for 15 minutes, giving the dish a half-turn, twice, during cooking.
7 Leave in container and stand, covered, for 20 minutes.
8 Turn out and, when quite cold, serve sprinkled with caster (superfine) sugar.
Serves 6–8.
Total Microwave Cooking Time: 15 minutes for each container

Note: This makes a delicious tea bread but can also be served hot, as a pudding with custard or cream.

Cherry Oat Cake

METRIC/IMPERIAL	AMERICAN
225g/8oz soft brown sugar	1⅓ cups light brown sugar
175g/6oz soft margarine	¾ cup soft margarine
50g/2oz glacé cherries, washed and chopped	¼ cup candied cherries, washed and chopped
100g/4oz raisins	1 cup raisins
50g/2oz rolled oats	½ cup rolled oats
1 teaspoon baking powder	1 teaspoon baking powder
pinch of salt	pinch of salt
50g/2oz mixed nuts, chopped	½ cup chopped mixed nuts
175g/6oz strong flour, wholemeal or white	1½ cups wholewheat bread flour
1 large egg	1 large egg
oil for greasing	oil for greasing
Optional Decoration:	Optional Decoration:
100g/4oz of cooking chocolate, melted	4 squares of cooking chocolate, melted
4 glacé cherries, halved	4 candied cherries, halved

1 Prepare an 18cm/7 inch soufflé dish by brushing the sides and base lightly with oil. Cut a circle of greaseproof paper (non-stick parchment) to fit the base and use a tablespoon of caster sugar to coat the sides. Do NOT apply more oil to base. Knock out any surplus sugar.
2 Place the sugar and margarine in a 1.75 litre/3 pint (7½ cup) mixing bowl, and microwave on POWER 7 for 3 minutes, until the margarine has melted. Stir well.
3 Stir in prepared cherries, raisins, rolled oats, baking powder, salt, mixed nuts and flour.
4 Mix well, then add the egg to combine the ingredients.
5 Pile the mixture into the prepared dish and level the top. Microwave on POWER 5 for 15 minutes.
6 Allow to stand in the container for 30 minutes before turning out onto a cooling rack.
7 When cool, spread the top with melted chocolate and decorate with cherries, if required.
Serves 8.
Total Microwave Cooking Time: 18 minutes (without chocolate)

Flapjacks

METRIC/IMPERIAL	AMERICAN
butter for greasing	butter for greasing
75g/3oz soft margarine	6 tablespoons soft margarine
75g/3oz soft dark brown sugar	½ cup dark brown sugar
1 tablespoon golden syrup	1 tablespoon light corn syrup
150g/5oz rolled oats	1½ cups rolled oats

1 Grease a 20cm/8 inch pie dish.
2 Put the margarine, sugar and syrup into a 1.75 litre/3 pint (7½ cup) ovenproof glass mixing bowl. Microwave on FULL POWER for 1½ minutes.
3 Add the oats, stirring them to coat them well.
4 Press oat mixture into the prepared pie dish.
5 Microwave on POWER 5 for 8 minutes, giving the dish a half-turn, twice, during cooking.
6 Cool for 10 minutes, then mark into fingers.
7 When cold, remove from the dish.
Makes 10.
Total Microwave Cooking Time: 9½ minutes
Variation
For chocolate flapjacks: Add 75g/3oz (3 squares) of chocolate, when melting the margarine.

Fruit and Walnut Cake

METRIC/IMPERIAL	AMERICAN
oil for greasing	oil for greasing
175g/6 oz self-raising flour	1½ cups self-rising flour
2 teaspoons mixed spice	2 teaspoons apple pie spice
175g/6oz soft margarine	¾ cup soft margarine
3 large eggs	3 large eggs
1 tablespoon milk	1 tablespoon milk
1 teaspoon liquid gravy browning	1 teaspoon liquid gravy coloring
175g/6oz soft brown sugar	1 cup light brown sugar
1 tablespoon black treacle	1 tablespoon molasses
100g/4oz mixed dried fruit	1 cup mixed dried fruit
25g/1oz walnuts, chopped	¼ cup chopped walnuts
a little caster sugar	a little superfine sugar

1 First, prepare a soufflé dish, 19cm/7½ inches in diameter, 10cm/4 inches deep. Lightly oil base of dish and line with a circle of greaseproof paper (non-stick parchment). DO NOT apply any more oil.
2 Use one stage method: put all the ingredients, except fruit and nuts, into a large mixing bowl. Mix to combine and beat for 2 minutes with a wooden spoon, or use an electric mixer.
3 Lightly fold in the fruit and nuts, then turn into the prepared dish.
4 Microwave on FULL POWER for 7–8 minutes.
5 Stand, covered, for 5 minutes. Turn out and, when quite cold, sprinkle top with caster (superfine) sugar.
Serves 8.
Total Microwave Cooking Time: 7–8 minutes

Shortbread Fingers

METRIC/IMPERIAL	AMERICAN
butter for greasing	butter for greasing
100g/4oz butter	½ cup butter
50g/2oz caster sugar	¼ cup sugar, firmly packed
175g/6oz plain flour	1½ cups all-purpose flour
½ teaspoon salt	½ teaspoon salt
caster sugar for sprinkling or 50g/2oz milk chocolate to coat	sugar for sprinkling or 2 squares chocolate to coat

1 Lightly grease a non-metallic shallow container 23 × 13 × 5cm/9 × 5 × 2 inch and sprinkle with flour, knocking out any surplus.
2 Combine the butter (straight from refrigerator) and sugar.
3 Gradually work in the flour and salt to form a pliable dough.
4 Press the dough into the prepared tin, using hands.
5 If possible, refrigerate for 20 minutes or freeze for 5 minutes. Prick well all over.
6 Microwave on POWER 8 for 5½ minutes, giving the dish a half-turn, twice, during cooking.
7 Allow to stand in the container for 10 minutes, then turn out onto a board.
8 Cut into fingers and, when quite cold, sprinkle with caster sugar (or follow 9, 10, 11).
9 Alternatively: while the shortbread is cooling, break the chocolate into pieces and place in a small ovenproof glass jug.
10 Microwave on POWER 3 for 3 minutes, then stir with a spoon.
11 When fully melted, spread over the shortbread. Allow to cool and set, and cut into fingers with a warm knife.
Serves 6–8.
Total Microwave Cooking Time: 5½ or 8 minutes

Shortbread Fingers (with caster sugar); Cherry Oat Cake; Flapjacks; Shortbread Fingers (with chocolate coating)

Wholemeal Plait

This recipe makes a large family-sized loaf. If preferred the dough can be halved at the end of Point 5 and two loaves can be shaped. Remember to halve the cooking time if the two loaves are cooked individually. White flour, or a mixture of brown and white flour, can be used.

METRIC/IMPERIAL	AMERICAN
1 teaspoon sugar	1 teaspoon sugar
300ml/½ pint tepid water	1¼ cups tepid water
1 teaspoon dried yeast	1 teaspoon active dry yeast
500g/1lb wholemeal flour	4 cups wholewheat flour
½ teaspoon salt	½ teaspoon salt
15g/½oz butter or margarine	1 tablespoon butter or margarine

1 Mix the sugar into one-third of the water in a small jug.
2 Sprinkle the dried yeast over the surface and leave in a warm place until frothy (about 10 minutes).
3 Place the flour and salt into a 1.75 litre/3 pint (7½ cup) mixing bowl, and microwave on FULL POWER for 30 seconds.
4 Rub the butter into the flour and add the yeast mixture and remaining tepid water. Mix well to form a pliable dough.
5 Turn onto a lightly floured board and knead until smooth (10 minutes).
6 To shape the loaf: divide the dough into three equal pieces. Roll and pull each piece into a 25cm/10 inch long roll. Join them together at one end and plait (braid) the loaf evenly. Finish by tucking the ends under.
7 Put onto a greased dinner plate and cover with a clean, damp tea (dish) towel. Leave in a warm place until dough has doubled in size (about 40 minutes).
8 Microwave, uncovered, on FULL POWER for 8 minutes, giving the plate a half-turn, half-way through cooking.
Serves 6.
Total Microwave Cooking Time: 8½ minutes

Note: Bread cooked in a microwave oven will not have the crisp crust of a loaf cooked conventionally. To crisp the loaf, put under a preheated hot grill (broiler) for 3—4 minutes after cooking. Allow to cool on a cooling rack, as usual.

Cup Cakes

METRIC/IMPERIAL	AMERICAN
2 large eggs	2 large eggs
100g/4oz caster sugar	½ cup sugar, firmly packed
100g/4oz self-raising flour	1 cup self-rising flour
100g/4oz soft margarine	½ cup soft margarine
2 tablespoons milk	2 tablespoons milk
2 tablespoons warm water	2 tablespoons warm water
175g/6oz icing sugar, sifted	1⅓ cups sifted confectioners' sugar
few drops of food colouring	few drops of food coloring
25g/1oz butter	2 tablespoons butter
coloured sugar strands to decorate	multicolored sprinkles to decorate

Nutty Gingerbread

METRIC/IMPERIAL	AMERICAN
melted butter for greasing	melted butter for greasing
a little caster sugar	a little superfine sugar
225g/8oz plain flour	2 cups all-purpose flour
½ teaspoon salt	½ teaspoon salt
1 teaspoon bicarbonate of soda	1 teaspoon baking soda
½ teaspoon mixed spice	½ teaspoon apple pie spice
2 teaspoons ground ginger	2 teaspoons ground ginger
100g/4oz soft brown sugar	⅔ cup light brown sugar
100g/4oz black treacle	⅓ cup molasses
100g/4oz margarine	½ cup margarine
100g/4oz golden syrup	⅓ cup light corn syrup
1 large egg, beaten	1 large egg, beaten
150ml/¼ pint milk	⅔ cup milk
25g/1oz mixed nuts, finely chopped	¼ cup mixed, finely chopped, nuts

Wholemeal Plait; Nutty Gingerbread; Cup Cakes

1 Put the eggs, sugar, flour, margarine and milk in a mixing bowl. Beat for 2 minutes with a wooden spoon to combine. Alternatively, use an electric mixer and beat for 1 minute.

2 Arrange 6 double cup cake cases in a ring on a dinner plate, leaving a gap in the centre. (This means using 2 cases for each cake: an alternative is to use a special microwave Muffin Pan which gives sufficient support, so that only one cake case needs to be used for each cake.)

3 Put 1 tablespoon of the mixture into each cake case and microwave on FULL POWER for 2 minutes.

4 Leave the cakes to rest for 1 minute, then turn onto a cooling rack and cool.

5 Continue with this method until all mixture has been used.

6 To make the icing: beat the water into the icing (confectioners') sugar. Beat in the colouring and butter, and use immediately to ice the cakes.

7 Decorate with coloured sugar strands.

Makes 18.
Total Microwave Cooking Time: 4½ minutes

1 Prepare a 23cm/9 inch ring mould: brush a little melted butter on the ring mould and sprinkle with caster (superfine) sugar — knock out any surplus.

2 Sift together the flour, salt, soda, spice and ginger.

3 Put the sugar, treacle (molasses), margarine and syrup in a large mixing bowl and microwave on POWER 7 for 3 minutes.

4 Stir well. Allow to cool slightly for 2–3 minutes.

5 Beat the egg and milk together, and add to the syrup mixture.

6 Make a well in centre of dry ingredients and add the liquid ingredients gradually, beating well to form a smooth batter.

7 Sprinkle chopped nuts evenly on base of the prepared mould, then pour in the cake batter.

8 Microwave on POWER 7 for 10–12 minutes, giving the dish a half-turn twice during cooking, if necessary.

9 Allow to cool in the dish for 10 minutes, then turn out and leave to cool completely.

Serves 6–8.
Total Microwave Cooking Time: 13 minutes
Variation
As an alternative, omit the nuts and coat the cooled gingerbread with glacé icing before cutting into slices.

Something Sweet

Although it may not be that much quicker to
make jams and sweets (candies) in a microwave oven
the whole operation is much simpler and cleaner.

JAM PREPARATION POINTS
To sterilize the jam jars: fill the jars two thirds full with cold
water and bring to the boil in the microwave oven.
Using oven gloves, remove the jars, empty and dry. To test for setting:
place a little of the boiled jam on a clean cold saucer.
Wait a minute or two then push your finger through the jam. The surface
will crinkle if setting point has been reached. If it does
not crinkle, boil the mixture for another minute or so and test again.

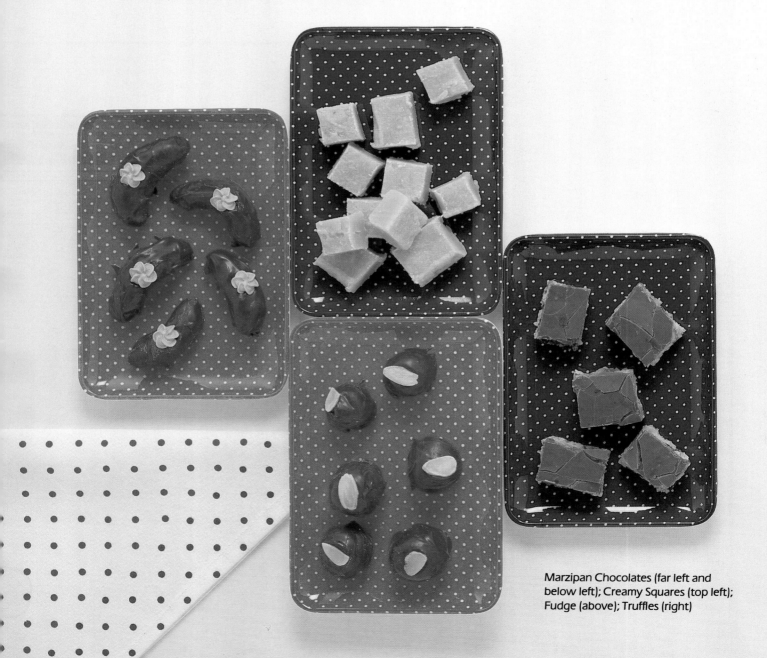

Marzipan Chocolates (far left and
below left); Creamy Squares (top left);
Fudge (above); Truffles (right)

Creamy Squares

METRIC/IMPERIAL	AMERICAN
200g/7oz cooking chocolate	7 squares semi-sweet chocolate
50g/2oz ground almonds	½ cup ground almonds
50g/2oz mixed dried fruit	½ cup mixed dried fruit
50g/2oz glacé cherries, washed and chopped	¼ cup candied cherries, washed and chopped
25g/1oz desiccated coconut	⅓ cup shredded coconut
50g/2oz caster sugar	¼ cup sugar, firmly packed
1 large egg, beaten	1 large egg, beaten

1 Break up the chocolate and put into the base of a clean 2.25 litre/4 pint (10 cup) ice cream container.
2 Microwave on POWER 3 for 5 minutes, stirring twice during cooking.
3 Spread over the base of the container to coat. Refrigerate for 10 minutes until set.
4 Mix all the dry ingredients together in a 1.75 litre/3 pint (7½ cup) mixing bowl. Bind with the beaten egg.
5 Spread the mixture over the set chocolate, evenly, pressing down with the back of a tablespoon.
6 Microwave on LOW POWER for 11 minutes.
7 Allow to cool in the container, then refrigerate. When chilled and firm, turn out and cut into tiny squares.
Makes 40.
Total Microwave Cooking Time: 16 minutes

Fudge

METRIC/IMPERIAL	AMERICAN
225g/8oz granulated sugar	2 cups sugar
225g/8oz caster sugar	¼ cup butter
50g/2oz butter	1¼ cups heavy cream
300ml/½ pint whipping cream	⅔ cup milk
150ml/¼ pint milk	1 teaspoon vanilla
1 teaspoon vanilla essence	

1 Put all the ingredients into a 2.25 litre/4 pint (10 cup) ovenproof mixing bowl, and stir well.
2 Microwave on POWER 7 for 7 minutes. Stir well to ensure that the sugar has dissolved. If the mixture still appears to be gritty, microwave for a further 2 minutes.
3 Return to microwave on FULL POWER and boil for 18 minutes. Stir twice during cooking.
4 Remove the bowl from the microwave and test with a sugar thermometer, which should reach 114°C/238°F within a minute or two.
5 Beat with a wooden spoon until the mixture becomes dull.
6 Pour into a well-greased 19 × 19 × 2.5cm/7½ × 7½ × 1 inch cake tin.
7 Leave to cool and refrigerate overnight to set. Cut into squares.
Serves 4.
Total Microwave Cooking Time: 25 minutes

Marzipan Chocolates

METRIC/IMPERIAL	AMERICAN
100g/4oz ready-made, good quality marzipan	¼lb ready-made, good quality marzipan
225g/8oz good quality plain or milk chocolate	½lb good quality semi-sweet chocolate .
a few flaked almonds, crystallized violets or sugar flowers	a few flaked almonds, candied violets or sugar flowers

1 Work the marzipan until pliable using your hands. Shape into small balls and small cigar shapes.
2 Place the chocolate in a 1.75 litre/3 pint (7½ cup) mixing bowl and microwave on POWER 3 for 6–7 minutes, stirring once. Beat until smooth.
3 Put a small amount of chocolate on the end of a round-bladed knife or palette knife. Position one piece of shaped marzipan on the chocolate, which will hold it in place. Spoon over the melted chocolate, to coat.
4 Leave on dinner plate to set and repeat until all the shapes have been coated.
5 Just before setting point is reached, decorate each marzipan chocolate with a piece of flaked almond, crystallized (candied) violet or sugar flower.
Makes about 12.
Total Microwave Cooking Time: 5 minutes

Truffles

METRIC/IMPERIAL	AMERICAN
100g/4oz plain chocolate	4 squares semi-sweet chocolate
1 egg yolk	1 egg yolk
15g/½oz butter	1 tablespoon butter
2 teaspoons sherry or rum	2 teaspoons sherry or rum
1 tablespoon single cream	1 tablespoon light cream
50g/2oz ground almonds	½ cup ground almonds
50g/2oz toasted almond nibs or chocolate vermicelli	½ cup toasted almond or chocolate sprinkles

1 Break the chocolate into pieces and place in a 1.75 litre/3 pint (7½ cup) mixing bowl.
2 Microwave on POWER 3 for 3–4 minutes, stirring once, half-way through cooking.
3 Beat in the egg yolk, butter, sherry, cream and ground almonds. Refrigerate for 10 minutes.
4 Shape into 12 balls, each the size of a walnut, and roll in the almonds or vermicelli.
5 Put the truffles into sweet paper cases and refrigerate.
Makes 12.
Total Microwave Cooking Time: 6 minutes

Quick and Easy Marmalade

METRIC/IMPERIAL	AMERICAN
1 × 875g/1lb 13oz can prepared Seville oranges	1 × 1lb 13oz can prepared Seville oranges
water (as directed on can)	water (as directed on can)
2kg/4lb granulated sugar	8 cups sugar, firmly packed
15g/½oz butter	1 tablespoon butter

1 Empty the contents of the can of oranges into a 2.25 litre/4 pint (10 cup) ovenproof mixing bowl, and stir in the water and sugar.
2 Microwave on FULL POWER for 4 minutes, and stir well.
3 Microwave on FULL POWER for 5–7 minutes, stirring with a wooden spoon every 2 minutes, until the sugar has dissolved.
4 Microwave on POWER 7 for 18–20 minutes, stirring twice during cooking. When stirring for the first time, stir in the butter.
5 To test for setting: Put a teaspoon of marmalade on a cold saucer. Allow to stand for 2 minutes, then push the surface with a finger. If the skin wrinkles then the marmalade is ready; if not microwave on FULL POWER for a further 1–2 minutes, and test again.
6 When setting point is reached, bottle in sterilized jars.
Yields 2.5kg/5½lb.
Total Microwave Cooking Time: 31 minutes

Candied Apples

METRIC/IMPERIAL	AMERICAN
175g/6oz soft brown sugar	1 cup light brown sugar
50g/2oz caster sugar	¼ cup sugar, firmly packed
25g/1oz margarine	2 tablespoons margarine
5 tablespoons water	5 tablespoons water
1 teaspoon vinegar	1 teaspoon vinegar
1 tablespoon golden syrup	1 tablespoon light corn syrup
4 wooden skewers	4 wooden skewers
4 firm, ripe eating apples, well washed and dried	4 firm, ripe eating apples, well washed and dried

1 Put the sugars, margarine, water, vinegar and syrup into a 1.75 litre/3 pint (7½ cup) mixing bowl, and stir.
2 Microwave on FULL POWER for 1 minute. Stir well for a few minutes to ensure that all the sugar has dissolved.
3 Return the bowl to the oven and Microwave on FULL POWER for 10 minutes, until a drop of toffee put into a mug of cold water hardens and cracks or breaks cleanly. A sugar thermometer should read 143°C/290°F but it must be used OUTSIDE the microwave oven.
4 Insert the skewers into the apples and dip each apple into the toffee, swirling it round until it is completely coated. Then plunge into cold water.
5 Leave the apples on a greased tray to set.
6 When set and cold, wrap each apple in plastic wrap or cellophane.
Makes 4.
Total Microwave Cooking Time: 11 minutes

Candied Apples;
Quick and Easy Marmalade;
Orange and Lemon Curd;
Raspberry Preserve

Raspberry Preserve

METRIC/IMPERIAL	AMERICAN
1kg/2lb freshly picked raspberries	6 cups freshly picked raspberries
1kg/2lb caster sugar	4 cups sugar, firmly packed

1 Do not wash the fruit. Place the raspberries in a 2.25–2.75 litre/4–5 pint (10–12 cup) mixing bowl, and crush them with the back of a wooden spoon.
2 Add the sugar. Cover the bowl with plastic wrap and leave in a cool place overnight.
3 Pierce the pastic wrap. Microwave on FULL POWER for 5 minutes and stir.
4 Microwave on POWER 7 for 24 minutes, stirring twice during cooking.
5 To test for setting: Put a little jam onto a cold saucer. Allow to cool for a minute or two and then push the jam with your finger. If the jam is ready, it will crinkle slightly.
6 Pot in sterilized jars, seal and cover.
Yields 1.5kg/3½lb.
Total Microwave Cooking Time: 29 minutes

Orange and Lemon Curd

METRIC/IMPERIAL	AMERICAN
2 medium-sized lemons, scrubbed	2 medium-sized lemons, scrubbed
2 medium-sized oranges, scrubbed	2 medium-sized oranges, scrubbed
225g/8oz unsalted butter, cut into pieces	1 cup unsalted butter, cut into pieces
500g/1lb granulated sugar	2 cups sugar, firmly packed
5 eggs, lightly beaten	5 eggs, lightly beaten

1 Arrange the fruit on a dinner plate and Microwave on FULL POWER for 1½ minutes.
2 Finely grate the rind from the fruit and put it into a 2.25 litre/4 pint (10 cup) mixing bowl.
3 Halve the fruits, and squeeze and strain juice into the bowl.
4 Add the butter and the sugar.
5 Microwave on POWER 6 for 7–8 minutes, stirring twice during cooking. Stir to ensure sugar has dissolved.
6 Strain the eggs into the bowl and beat well with a wooden spoon.
7 Return the bowl to the microwave oven and heat on POWER 5 for about 15 minutes, stirring every 2 minutes during cooking, until the mixture coats the back of the spoon.
8 Put in sterilized jars and seal.
Yields about 1.25kg/2½lb.
Total Microwave Cooking Time: 24½ minutes

ROASTING MEAT

Selected cuts of meat may be cooked in a remarkably short time in the microwave oven. As with a conventional oven, the cooking times are determined by the weight of the meat. Use the following cooking chart to determine cooking times for the various kinds of meat.

Joints of meat cook more evenly if they are boned and rolled. (This is because bone is a good conductor of heat and meat close to the bone will overcook.) Place the meat in the roasting bag (with or without added ingredients) and secure with a rubber band. Pierce the base of the bag to allow steam to escape and meat juices to flow out into the cooking utensil, (these juices can be used later for gravy). Then place the bag on a non metallic rack or an upturned saucer in a non metallic cooking dish.

It is advisable to use a microwave meat thermometer (or the temperature probe of the microwave oven) to gauge the proper degree of doneness. Insert the thermometer into the thickest part of the meat. When the required temperature has been reached, allow the meat to stand, out of the microwave oven, loosely covered with a 'tent' of aluminium foil, for 15 to 20 minutes so that the temperature of the meat equalizes throughout. During this standing time the thermometer should indicate an increase of 10 to 15°F (5 to 7°C).

If you prefer, you can cook meat on FULL POWER for a few minutes but then complete the cooking on POWER 8. Increase total cooking time by 1 minute per lb (500g).

Type of Meat	Approximate Cooking Time per pound on Full Power		Internal Temperature After Cooking		Internal Temperature After Standing	
Beef off the bone	Rare	5–6 mins	57°C	130°F	62°C	140°F
	Medium	7–8 mins	65°C	150°F	70°C	160°F
	Well done	8–10 mins	73°C	160°F	78°C	170°F
Beef on the bone	Rare	5 mins	57°C	130°F	62°C	140°F
	Medium	6 mins	65°C	150°F	70°C	160°F
	Well done	8 mins	73°C	160°F	78°C	170°F
Poultry	7 mins per 500g/1lb		85°C	185°F	94°C	190°F
Veal	8–9 mins per 500g/1lb		73°C	160°F	78°C	170°F
Pork	9–10 mins per 500g/1lb		80°C	180°F	85°C	190°F
Lamb	8–9 mins per 500g/1lb		77°C	170°F	82°C	180°F
Ham	6 mins per 500g/1lb		77°C	170°F	82°C	180°F

DEFROSTING

The microwave oven and the freezer are a natural team since the defrost feature rapidly thaws frozen food. But there are a few points to remember...

Before defrosting, pierce the freezer bag or loosen the container lid to allow steam to escape. Transfer food from foil containers to plastic or glass dishes if necessary. Most foods need to be turned or re-arranged during the defrost cycle. Always remove the bag of giblets from the body cavity of whole chickens and small turkeys before the bird is stored in the freezer. Cook giblets separately for use in gravies or stuffings.

When defrosting foods that are not of uniform size, for example a whole fish or chicken, the thinner areas are likely to start to cook before the thicker parts have completely defrosted so it is a good idea to mask parts like the fish tail or chicken wing with a small amount of foil; this foil repels the microwaves and prevents these thin areas from becoming dry and overcooked. FOLLOW THESE INSTRUCTIONS ONLY IF THE MANUFACTURERS OF YOUR MICROWAVE OVEN PERMITS THE USE OF SMALL AMOUNTS OF FOIL.

Frozen vegetables can be cooked straight from the freezer but all other foods should be allowed to stand after defrosting and before cooking. Standing time will vary from 5 to 15 minutes depending on the amount and density of the food. It is best to defrost delicate foods like cream filled sponges, mousses and cheesecakes for a very short time only then leave at room temperature or in the refrigerator to thaw completely.

SOME USEFUL DEFROST TIMES

Food and Weight	Special Instructions	Time
500g/1lb fish	Turn over once	9 mins.
225g/½lb prawns (shrimp)	Stir once	5 mins.
1 large loaf	Finish at room temperature	5 mins.
6 small cakes	Rearrange once	3 mins.
350g/¾lb sponge cake		3 mins.
500g/lb chops or chicken pieces	Rearrange once	8 mins.
500g/1lb savoury flan		3 mins
500g/1lb fruit	Stir once	5 mins.
225g/½lb cooked rice	Break up with fork once	3 mins.
225g/½lb butter or margarine		3 mins.
750g/1½lb prepared casserole	Stir once	12 mins.
Plated meal		5 mins.
750g/1½lb prepared lasagne or cooked meat dish	Turn dish once	18 mins.
500g/1lb cuts of meat or poultry	Halfway through cooking shield any warm area with a little foil. Turn meat over once	4–5 mins.
500g/1lb sausages	Separate sausages as soon as possible and rearrange	5–6 mins.

REHEATING FOODS

The microwave oven is extremely helpful for fast, efficient reheating, saving on both fuel and washing up. Meat and poultry can be reheated safely because the intense internal temperature reached within the food eliminates the danger of food poisoning. A plated meal, covered with plastic wrap to prevent dehydration, can be reheated in 3 to 4 minutes. Various canned foods, such as baked beans and spaghetti, can be reheated at the same time if transferred to separate bowls. Pastry and dough products like pies and pizzas can also be reheated within minutes and if the resulting hot product appears a bit too moist, crisp it under a preheated conventional grill (broiler).

When reheating bread products, such as rolls or loaves of bread, wrap them first in absorbent kitchen towelling.

Almost any dish may be prepared in the morning (or the day before) for evening meal reheating. Indeed, meat dishes often taste better if their flavour is allowed to develop for several hours before serving.

Reheat delicate sauces containing cream and egg yolks on power 4 or 5 to prevent curdling.

NOTE: Unless otherwise stated food to be reheated should be covered with plastic wrap to prevent dehydration. Pierce the wrap in several places to allow steam to escape.

Certain foods, like stews and casseroles, should be stirred during reheating to ensure even heat distribution.

After reheating, remove food from the microwave oven and allow to stand for a few minutes before serving.

REHEATING COOKED FOODS

Food and Weight	Special Instructions	Time	Power
400g/14oz can vegetables	Drain and transfer to a non-metallic container	3 mins.	Full
2 servings stew or casserole		5 mins.	Power 8
1 plated meal of meat and two vegetables		4 mins.	Full
6 sausages (links) or frankfurters	Rearrange once to ensure even cooking	2½ mins.	Full
500g/1lb savoury dish like lasagne or spaghetti bolognese		7 mins.	Full
2 chicken portions		4 mins.	Full
2 servings of prepared dessert (pies, crumbles etc)	Do not cover	1 min.	Full
225g/½lb rice or pasta		2 mins.	Full
200g/7oz canned savoury food	Transfer to a non-metallic container	2 mins.	Power 7
300ml/½ pint (¾ cup) sauce or custard	Stir once	3–4 mins.	Power 8
4 beefburgers (500g/1lb total)		2 mins.	Power 8
500g/1lb vegetables		3 mins.	Full

VEGETABLE COOKING CHART

Cook fresh or frozen vegetables in a covered container or pierced roasting or freezing bag sealed with a rubber band, turn once halfway through the cooking time. Frozen vegetables can be cooked in their plastic packets but remember to pierce several times to allow the steam to escape. Cooking times for fresh vegetables will vary slightly depending upon the freshness, age and temperature of the vegetable. Both fresh and frozen vegetables will need a standing time of 3 to 5 minutes after cooking, this will depend upon the density of the vegetable.

Vegetable	Weight	Additions	Approximate Cooking Time on Full Power	Special Instructions
Asparagus FRESH	500g/1lb	3 tablespoons cold water	7 mins.	Stir once
Asparagus FROZEN	350g/¾lb	25g/1oz (2 tablespoons butter)—no water	7 mins.	Rearrange once
Beans, Broad FRESH	225g/½lb prepared beans	2 tablespoons cold water	4–5 mins.	Stir once
Beans, Broad (Lima) FROZEN	225g/½lb	1 tablespoon cold water	6–7 mins.	Stir once
Beans, Green sliced, FRESH	500g/1lb	2 tablespoons cold water	11 mins.	Stir once
Beans, Green sliced, FROZEN	225g/½lb	2 tablespoons cold water	5 mins	Stir once
Broccoli FRESH	500g/1lb	3 tablespoons cold water	8 mins.	Stir once
Broccoli FROZEN	225g/½lb	1 tablespoon cold water	6 mins.	Rearrange once
Brussels Sprouts FRESH	225g/½lb prepared sprouts	2 tablespoons cold water	4 mins.	Stir once
Brussels Sprouts FROZEN	225g/½lb	1 tablespoon cold water	3½ mins.	Rearrange once
Cabbage, shredded FRESH	500g/1lb	¼ pint boiling water	10 mins.	Stir once
Carrots, sliced FRESH	500g/1lb	3 tablespoons cold water	8 mins. new; 10 mins. old	Stir once

Vegetable	Weight	Additions	Approximate Cooking Time on Full Power	Special Instructions
Carrots, sliced FROZEN	225g/½lb	2 tablespoons cold water	6 mins.	Rearrange once
Cauliflower florets FRESH	500g/1lb	3 tablespoons cold water	7 mins.	Stir once
Cauliflower florets FROZEN	225g/½lb	1 tablespoon cold water	6 mins.	Rearrange once
Corn On The Cob FRESH	2 cobs	25g/1oz (2 tablespoons) butter	6 mins.	Turn once
Corn kernels FROZEN	225g/½lb	25g/1oz (2 tablespoons) butter—no water	3 mins.	Turn once
Courgettes (Zucchini), sliced FRESH	500g/1lb	No water	6 mins.	Stir once
Mushrooms, sliced FRESH	225g/½lb	25g/1oz (2 tablespoons) butter—no water	2 mins.	Stir once
Peas FRESH	500g/1lb	2 tablespoons water	5 mins.	Stir once
Peas FROZEN	225g/½lb	25g/1oz (2 tablespoons butter)—no water	4 mins.	Stir once
Potatoes, quartered FRESH	500g/1lb	OLD—3 tablespoons cold water NEW—1 tablespoon cold water	old—9 mins. new—7 mins.	
Spinach FRESH	500g/1lb	no water	6 mins.	
Spinach FROZEN	225g/½lb		5 mins.	Stir once

Index

Special photography by Charlie
Stebbings